OF BULLETS, BOMBS, AND ARMORED CARS, MY LIFE ADVENTURES

OF BULLETS, BOMBS, AND ARMORED CARS, MY LIFE ADVENTURES

(A TRUE JAMES-BOND STYLE OF STORY.)
(AND A STORY OF THE FIRST US SPACECRAFT.)

Scott J. Harden

Copyright © 2017 by Scott J. Harden.

Library of Congress Control Number: 2017903050
ISBN: Hardcover   978-1-5245-8775-8
                   Softcover   978-1-5245-8774-1
                   eBook   978-1-5245-8773-4

All rights reserved. No part of this book may be reproduced or transmitted in any form or by any means, electronic or mechanical, including photocopying, recording, or by any information storage and retrieval system, without permission in writing from the copyright owner.

Any people depicted in stock imagery provided by Thinkstock are models, and such images are being used for illustrative purposes only.
Certain stock imagery © Thinkstock.

Print information available on the last page.

Rev. date: 03/10/2017

To order additional copies of this book, contact:
Xlibris
1-888-795-4274
www.Xlibris.com
Orders@Xlibris.com
753304

CONTENTS

Introduction vii

1	Living in a Cabin	1
2	Taken Prisoner	3
3	Morgue Stories	6
4	Murderous Politics	11
5	Crooked Nose	14
6	Wild Child	16
7	Ships Officer	20
8	Alone in the Jungle	26
9	Life at Sea and Similar Tales	31
10	Part Time Soldier of Fortune	37
11	Married under Questionable Circumstances ...	44
12	School Again	50
13	The First Satellites	54
14	Back to the South American	61
15	Off to South America	65
16	Itty Bitty Things	73
17	Outer Space Research	79
18	Insanity Raises it's Ugly Head, Again	86
19	Alaska and the Oil Rush	94
20	Murder, Almost	113
21	More "Spacy" Things	116
22	Voice of America	118
23	Flight to Alaska	126
24	Life as a Bush Rat	129
25	Small Island in the Atlantic	135
26	A Canadian Russian Town	138
27	Moving back to USA	140

INTRODUCTION

I HAVE WORKED IN twenty countries now and have been paid by branches of the Department of Defence and the Central Intelligence Agency. My life sometimes resembled Kurt Strong. But I also married a psychotic woman and real life was often a live action version of a fictional soap opera set in Hell. Between all this activity I made my homes on the Beltway in Washington, D.C., the high mountains of Colorado, and a lake in Alaska among other places. I have been the builder of the first satellites, a helicopter pilot, navigator, ship's officer, small arms instructor, president of a gambling corporation, and a lot of other things. People keep asking me to write up my life... well here it is on a platter...

1
LIVING IN A CABIN

ONE OF MY earliest memories today is living in a rustic cabin in the mountains west of New York City. My mother, Jennifer May Cardoza, had been assistant and nurse to the exceedingly rich Rosen family. I don't know all the facts but apparently there was a death in the family and my mother was out of a job. After that she married my father Kurt Harden, a medical doctor and researcher. I came along, and so did the Great Depression of the 1930's. With work hard to find, even in the medical profession, my parents moved to Syracuse, New York in the United States.

I was born on September 28, 1930 in "up state" New York. My folks had built a house on Scott Avenue, in Syracuse, and just almost finished it with pre depression money they had saved. Both my folks had to do whatever they could to provide income, eat and to pay for the house. Dad started a pediatric medical practice, but most of his patients had trouble paying. He also worked for a University Medical School as a professor and for the City of Syracuse coroner's office. At four years old my mother would take me and my two year old sister Janet to a Girl Scout camp for the summer. She was camp nurse.

This encampment was in the Catskill Mountains west of New York City. In those days it seemed to me to be a remote, wild, wilderness. A dirt road lead into the place and visiting cars were very rare. We lived in a slab sided wood cabin. A rustic cabin made of very

1

rough cut boards and never painted. As I remember it was on a hill above the mess hall where we would eat all our meals.

The girls were always very good to me. Even the cook, Bonnie, always had something for me in the kitchen. Bonnie cooked over a wood stove and had to split all the wood herself. One day her ax missed the mark and she chopped her leg. I had a hard time understanding why Bonnie had no goodies for me, and my mother had no time for me either.

This kind of accident was rare and Bonnie did survive, but she was much more careful with the ax as I remember. We kids never got to spend much time in the Clinic so my memories are scarce of my mother's work.

Janet and I spent much of our time learning to swim. Really it was pushing a float and wearing water wings. Later on Dad took us both out to the Indian Reservation adjacent to the farm where he had grown up, and he taught us how to really swim.

During the summers at camp we were surrounded by thick trees with sunlight and shadows. At night there were no windows but we did have a screen to keep out the mosquitoes. Also at night I still remember hearing the deer come up on our rustic porch and clomp out their greetings with their hooves. At night I could hear the girls sit around the camp fire and singing songs like "The Ash Grove" from Wales. I think this kind of life and the memories of it influenced the remainder of my life. It gave me the love of the woods and a special love of Welch music the girls would sing. Perhaps this part of my life drove me to wander the world to search another "forest primeval" or perhaps it was other things, you be the judge.

2

TAKEN PRISONER

I LIVED NEAR THE city limits of Syracuse, New York, in the United States. Behind our house were glacial hills called drumlins, and some were covered with forest. As a boy I had a good time wandering about over these hills and playing with my friends around the ponds and in the hard wood forests. We spent many days trying to shoot dragon flies with our BB guns, expending thousands of BB on entirely futile target practice. I also liked to be around the cows in the fenced areas of these hills and learned to moo like a cow. I learned that cows do indeed say things with the tone of the moo, like "child, where are you?", or "hey everyone, I have just found a hole in the fence, lets all run away!" I got pretty good at imitating the various "moo" words, and could get the whole herd to come running to where they thought there might be a hole in the fence. Luckily the farmer never noticed how his cows would run way off now and then. Those were mostly warm and enjoyable days.

There was a large country club that had been built in the forest on a hill top behind our house. Before completion the economic depression of 1929 hit and work was stopped on the country club house and it was deserted. At that point a family called Ash moved in to the place. They had lots of kids close to my age, and the old club had lots of space for bedrooms. It was mostly unheated in winter, except for the coal stove in the kitchen. I can remember spending a lot of time with Brian, Mary, and Joan Ash in their warm kitchen.

I was shocked to find that they often had little to eat except bread covered with mustard, or rabbits they shot in the woods. The Ash children, however, were experts at finding anything eatable in the forest. So I also learned where to find wild grapes, or abandoned apple trees, or any thing else that could be eaten.

One day all my friends on the hill top got in their jalopy automobile and left for the promised land of California. It was sad and I never heard of any of them again. Two weeks after they left the old country club house burned to the ground and erased an episode of my life.

Other strange things happened in the hills. A number of neighbour children would also wander about in the forest and local cow pastures. One day we learned what it was to be a hostage, or a prisoner. Several of my friends and I were walking about near "the pond" where the cows drank. We were approached by two men with a rifle. The men said "alright all of you get together in a bunch" and they pointed the rifle at us.

None of us had any experience with this sort of treatment but we did as we were told. We sat on the ground for perhaps an hour or two wile the two men grilled us on where we lived, and why we were in the woods. "Alright tell us where you live and how far away it is, or else!" We were not quite sure of what that meant, but it sounded ominous.

Every so often one of the men would load the rifle and shoot at something, perhaps a tree, or perhaps a rock. Never much purpose that I could see, except I did notice that the rifle was very temperamental and demanding. Finally one of my friends, a girl named Jennifer, who was a little older and very demanding shouted out "You can't do this. You can't keep us prisoner here! I'm leaving!"

With this the man with the gun loaded it, and I could see that as I was right next to him. He put the gun muzzle in the girl's stomach and pulled the trigger. It didn't fire! He reloaded the rifle again and pulled the trigger with it still pressed tightly against Jennifer's stomach. And again it didn't fire! The man turned livid and white in the face going into an insane furry. He exactly repeated his action in loading the cartridge and closing the bolt, but this time he pointed the rifle at a small piece of glass near his foot, and it fired! The glass dissolved in a shower of glistening particles, and suddenly the man changed from livid anger to a smiling mask.

At this point in time one of my boy friends, Greg, decided he had enough of being a prisoner and he decided to run for it. He ran as fast as he could down hill through the pasture with bullets kicking up dirt all around him. Finally when he was about 100 yards away he fell and remained quiet. We didn't know if he had been hit or what had happened.

After some minutes Greg slowly got up and slowly came back to our group. He didn't know what was going to happen to him I found out later. Perhaps they were going to kill him for trying to escape, or who knows what. He kept very quiet from then on, and so did Jennifer.

To me a most remarkable thing happened at this point. The two men got to arguing about some small thing that had happened to them recently and they just seemed to forget about us. The rifle was pointed away from our little band of children. We just quickly wandered away from the men taking the most invisible route possible back to our homes.

Naturally I, and everyone else, reported to their parents what had happened. The police were called. We found out that the two men had escaped from an insane asylum and stolen a rifle along the way. They then disappeared into the woods. We knew what happened then, they found us and held us prisoner. But the story ends when the police captured the two men and we presumed returned them to a more secure asylum.

MORGUE STORIES

AS ECONOMIC TIMES got a bit better my mother and dad started having servants live-in at our house. Mother always seemed to assume that everyone had servants to do the work too or it seemed to me that is the way she thought. Of course mother had come from a family where servants were normal and she herself had been brought up by "Barbarita" speaking Mexican Spanish on the Rio Grand River.

My mother's father had been a promoter of Italian singing stars in Mexico. Remember that was the days before records, radio, and television. He traveled extensively and worked entirely in Spanish. Her mother had a French background from Canada. Indeed I can remember having mother tell me, very confidentially, that English was a bad language and that French was The Language. But that was when I was perhaps four. After that she seldom talked of French again, but she did speak Spanish from time to time. Indeed she taught me revolutionary songs from Mexico as a child but they had little meaning to me.

Grandfather Cardoza decided to go into the oil business about 1902. It was the "big thing" in that day and people were getting rich. Spindle Top Bayou had lots of oil and the Cardoza Oil Company hit it big! But those were ruthless days and there were ruthless competitors. His oil tank cars were side tracked purposely by the rail roads owned by John Rock. He could not get his oil to market. Then real disaster hit.

Fire! Someone set fire to the Cardoza Oil Company oil wells. The remainder of the oil field burned too, all except the part belonging to John Rock. All this was printed in the Oil Investors Journal about 1904.

Then more disaster hit grandfather Frank Cardoza too. His wife died in Texas of yellow fever. The double disaster hit grandfather below the belt. He took his three children, Barbara, Tom, and David, to Indiana where he had relatives. He himself became very religious and campaigned against drink with religious fervor. Somehow he became a promoter for a popular public speaker of the day, named Peter Rivers Peters, on his extensive religious trip through Alaska.

Grandfather had met the daughter of an Indiana druggist of Canadian persuasion (A. B. French, of River John, Nova Scotia). She never used her real French name as it seemed embarrassing to her, so she simply became "Browne" French. In any case the two were married in Seattle, Washington on the way to Alaska.

In Alaska the two met all the famous people of their day as they wandered through almost every bit of Alaska and the Canadian Klondike gold fields. Indeed grandfather visited with a bank clerk in his log cabin house at Dawson to read his poetry. Robert Service asked if his poems were any good. Grandfather said he thought that they certainly could be published, and told him how to get them published. At least that is how the Associated Press put it in 1936 after Service became famous.

Grandmother "Browne" appropriately was an expert with the Kodak "Browne" camera and took many photographs of the arctic Alaskan trip. These were to be the basis of their income for many years to come as Frank used these as part of his "Chautauqua" lecture circuit series and part of his book on Alaska called "Wolf the Storm Leader". However because grandmother was pregnant with my mother, Jennifer May, they suddenly left western Alaska by steam ship for Seattle.

A few years later Frank Cardoza was promoting farm land purchases along the Rio Grand River, Texas often to farmers from Indiana. He would move a whole train load of farmers down to the border at a time. In the mean time his family, now expanded, grew up on the Mexican border. Only trouble with that was that there was a political revolution going on in Mexico and it burst across the border. Poncho Villa (his original name was Doroteo Arango) was well known. Villa had a great hate for the president of the United States, William Harden. This was due to Harden's successful attempt to split allegiances in Mexico. As commonly avoided in U.S. history books the Villa guerrilla fighters actually attacked into Texas again and again. There were continual battles and even mass killings that were seldom reported. I personally ran into this bloody history in Texas. Anyway the Cardoza's were in the middle.

My mother told me of armed men keeping guard on their house all night. She and her brothers and sisters dressed in black so they could hide in the mesquite brush out of sight of the raiders. The dinner table talk according to aunt Barbara was always who got killed today. She had taught in a Mexican school. Her brother David also told me that he took a job as body guard for a Mexican jeweler, but that his client was killed right behind him thus ending his job. He also showed me photographs he had taken of a passenger train in Texas that had been derailed and all the men aboard killed. He had been the first to get to the train after the guerrillas and all the bodies were in his pictures. Life in Texas during The Mexican Revolution was bad.

Frank Cardoza decided to move his family north to El Dorado, Kansas, where they would be more safe. From here my mother Jennifer May went to New York City to study to be a nurse at Mount Sinai Hospital.

In New York Jennifer May met Dr. Kurt Robert Harden, an early vitamin "A" researcher. Their common interest seem to be that both their parents were involved in the anti-alcohol campaigns of the 1920's.

Kurt Harden grew up as the only child on a farm near Hanover Center, New York, in the westernmost part of New York State. His father practiced Scottish birth control, which is waiting until you are 50 or so to marry! Kurt did have a person he fully considered a sister, Ruby, the daughter of an itinerant house painter who simply dropped her off at their house, where she remained for years. Suddenly one day the painter returned and Ruby was gone forever, without a trace.

His father Henry Harden had obtained the farm from his father, Kurt Harden, who apparently had purchased it from the Hudson's Bay Company after arriving from Scotland. The farm was devoted to grape growing and it was highly successful. Of course being a prohibitionist Henry Harden only grew "new world" grapes which made really bad wine! The family retired to Bradenton, Florida about 1910. Later on they moved to Sebring, Florida in the center of the Florida peninsula.

Back in Syracuse Dr. Kurt Harden had to work extra hours to make ends meet and finish paying for that new house on Scott Avenue. He had studied vitamin A deficiency at Harvard Medical School and had done a lot of autopsy work. This gave him three extra jobs with income during the big depression. First he went to work for the Walnut Package Company designing high quality baby foods, the kind that come in a small jar today. Next he taught dissection of human bodies at the local medical school. And lastly he was on call by the City of Syracuse to do autopsies on various bodies of "interest", particularly to the police.

Now you should know that Jennifer May believed that a family, even children, should all eat together in formal fashion. Thus each evening when Dad came home we would dress for dinner and go to the formal dining room. The servants, if there were any at the moment, would bring in the dinner. Children were expected to listen to the adult conversations and only comment briefly. Well that is what I did, and did it help me out later in ways I never would have expected.

Being conversation between a doctor and a nurse gave a definite medical color to the conversations. Dad would usually discuss the autopsy of the day. Boy was this fascinating for a kid! I would hear about who was shot and what it would do, who was hit over the head with a bottle and why it killed him, why Mrs. X actually died of all the strange illnesses that were put down to her being a "hypochondriac", then there was the power line technician who let the cable slip and it went through his eye and killed him. Of course these are just a few of the cases discussed in detail at the dinning table. I thought everyone had dinner conversations like this at home!

Now if you haven't become ill I will tell you how this benefited me. My mother also thought (don't ask me why) that boys and girls should all be able to make their own school lunches. Mine were always peanut butter and jam sandwiches. But being a bit lazy I would forget to make my sandwiches some days, or perhaps I would skimp a bit and make really bad sandwiches. Well this could be remedied easily.

Sitting in the school cafeteria with my various buddies I would spy some especially good lunch across the table. Something made with love by his mother no doubt. Well, I would begin to tell the truly awful morgue stories I had heard at my dinning room table. My eye was very good in catching how far I should go to get my mates to abandon their luncheon. As for me, I ate very well every school day! But school was not all fun and games by any means.

MURDEROUS POLITICS

MY MOTHER, JENNIFER May, had a great interest in politics. I don't really know where this came from, perhaps from her father Frank Cardoza. Mother had told me a little of the politics of the Mexican Revolution, and how her father had met with one of the well known Communist Russian leaders exiled in Mexico before he was assassinated. Grandfather had also rescued one of the prominent Mexican generals after he was shot in a big battle. So I guess the seed of politics was planted in fertile ground.

Syracuse, New York, was an industrial town in those days. Shortly before the great depression of the 1930s it drew workers from all over Europe in large numbers. Of course the Irish had come to build the Erie Canal even earlier. The city was full of many people, many still speaking their original languages, particularly people from Italy and Sicily. They were a tough crowd.

Mother jumped right into the middle of the local political scene which was apparently controlled by Mayor Scadente and his law partner Mr. Deutscher. She was also was involved in U.S. national politics too. As a child she had me parading up and down as a sandwich man with advertising for the presidential hopefuls. We received bag after bag of mail at the house which mother and her friends would sort and answer. But no matter what it seemed to me that President Roosevelt always won the national elections.

This led on into the convoluted world of local politics. I remember that mother became the elected head of "Organized Women" (O.W.). This grew quickly to an organization of about 10,000 women and mother was president. O.W. was considered a very radical Union organization by the established politicians because O.W. had great power to elect officials, and that power was clearly not under the control of the men politicians. Remember in those days women had just barely gained the right to vote and women were considered very dangerous and unreliable to the establishment.

All this time I was learning politics at my mother's knee. I learned the nasty and seamy sides of political officials. I learned how votes could be bought and sold. How pay offs were made outside the voting booths. How pressure was put on people to "vote right". How a single speech could effect the outcome of an entire election. Things that are still being learned by people looking to be elected.

Mother gave many speeches in public and on the radio in those days. However, she met a much more dynamic speaker Judy Hall. Mother and Mrs. Hall worked well together. Mother wrote the radio speeches and Judy gave them on the radio. They were a highly effective pair. Mother was ecstatic over their success in influencing the politics of Syracuse, New York.

There was much going on that I didn't hear I am sure. My mother was never paranoid about anything, until strange things started happening. One of the lawyers who worked with Organized Women simply disappeared off the street and was never heard from again! I can remember asking about him several times, but the answer was always negative.

We could often hear strange "clicks" on the telephone at home. Apparently our telephone was being "tapped", but "they" did not want to listen to the talk of children. After this mother did seem paranoid about talking on the telephone. It bothered me.

My father was teaching at the Medical School. Suddenly the University was told that the University would have to start paying taxes, lots more taxes, if Mrs. Harden did not quit politics. I heard little more of this ploy, but apparently mother had some solution to the problem.

Well after that the "other side" got rougher, and I was in the middle. One day I was playing with several friends in the tall grass behind our house. I noticed a man with a telescoped rifle siting on the hill behind the house and point his gun my way. The next thing I remember was the grass folding over right next to my leg along the path of the bullet. I was the target! Not being dumb I ran over behind a large tree. It was my luck that one of my friends was playing near by.

I shouted to my friend to run to my house and tell them what was going on. Guy Hagaman did as instructed. I stuck my head out quickly to see if the sniper had gone and wham a bullet hit the tree at head height. Pretty soon a car came bounding up the adjacent dirt road at a great speed and dad called to me. I ran for the presumed safety of the car and we headed out at a great speed. It was thus I learned first hand about indirect political pressure and assassination.

5

CROOKED NOSE

AT LEAST THE assassin missed with a three shots this time and I felt real lucky. Things like that get a kid to thinking about his mortality. But there were a few other hard times too.

Take for example the day when I was running at full speed during an improvised gym session. Well I slipped and as I was falling Robert Sherman's leg was coming up. It caught me right on the nose.

Probably I was at some disadvantage having only one eye functioning. From birth my right eye was dysfunctional. Still I was never going to let this keep me from anything the other boys might do. I never thought much about not having the same vision as the other boys, but now and then it did catch up with me.

Next thing I knew was slowly becoming aware of the world around me and that I was on a couch in the school nurse's office. My nose hurt pretty bad and someone held up a mirror so that I could see. My nose was on my right cheek.

With one hand I straightened out my nose to the best of my ability. Then I must have sort of passed out again. It took perhaps 24 hours to regain full awareness of the world around me. Someone picked me up and took me home.

For the remainder of my life my nose has had a list to the right. Each physician I visit seems to discover that fact and ask me if I knew about it. The answer was always "sure". But like all kids, I guess, there were other accidents.

Take for example the time in camp when I was a Junior Councillor. My whole cabin crew decided to beat me up, just for the hell of it. Naturally I was about 6 inches taller than any of the others so I expected I could easily win against all 12 boys, at least when taken one at a time. Well it worked pretty good for the first ten, then I was pretty tuckered out. The eleventh boy was tough as the devil and grabbed me by the head and started beating my head on the floor.

Some time later I came to and everyone was gone. I found out later they thought that they had killed me and all headed for the woods. In the mean time I took a good long swim in the cold lake water to revive. But the effects of the beating actually took many months to wear off. I learned that protecting the head is the second most important part of fighting! The most important thing is to use your head first!.

WILD CHILD

BY THE TIME I was in New Hall High School at Winnetka, Illinois I was doing quite as I wanted to do. As far as the academics of school were concerned, well there was little fun in that. And very honestly I was an awful student. But I loved the special tests, unlike almost everyone else in the school. I loved to work too and worked at Gunns TV repair shop every day after school making in those days the princely sum of $75. dollars a week. Amateur radio also fascinated me as I was good at it, I could talk to people all over the world, and I became president of the high school radio club. Little did I know what would come of this. Most of all I loved all the girls in high school and spent every moment I could at dances and social functions. What red blooded boy full of hormones could avoid this kind of life?

My family had moved very suddenly from Syracuse to the suburbs of Chicago after my assassination attempt. I spent a few months living with the industrialist Van Wagnen family in a remote part of Syracuse. Mother and my three sisters moved to Silver Creek, New York until dad could buy a house in Illinois. Dad had suddenly acquired a new position as the Secretary of the Foods and Nutrition Board of the American Medical Association.

In Chicago mother made one or two weak attempts to join the politics of the City. After one such meeting in the city there was some guarded heavy discussions between mother and dad. She decided that it wasn't safe to go into big city politics, particularly in the home ground of the well known Midwest Italian Malia! I couldn't hear what was said but apparently dad agreed.

Again we had servants to do the work and mother simply had to find something to occupy her time. She started writing for "Today's Health" magazine, and she started designing kitchens for the rich and famous of Chicago.

This left me mostly on my own. I avoided learning how to drive unlike all the other kids. I knew, with a great certainty, that I would become my mother's full time "go-fer" supporting her kitchen business. When I did get my drivers license this prediction turned out to be 100% correct. My work at Gunns was finished and my private income was now zero. Inexplicably mother never paid a penny for that kind of labor.

For some reason I never fully understood mother made Janet and I take dance lessons from a Mrs. Willson. She had large classes with a hundred or so students. I had to dance with my sister, yecch!!! This was almost the worst thing that could possibly happen to a teen age boy!

Back in high school we were all sorted out alphabetically. I sat next to Donna Paine in one study hall and in a class or two. We started going to all the local dances together, and it was a lot of fun. Perhaps mother did have some pity on me after all. Knowing how to dance let me date all sorts of girls, but Donna was my favorite. After more than fifty years I still wonder what happened to her.

I had never thought seriously of going on to college. However ninety eight percent of the students in my high school did go, but I just never thought about it. Perhaps it was because my parents were always so busy with their own lives they never had much time to talk to me about why I should go to college.

Suddenly in September I was sent, all alone, 500 miles east to Angeles College at Meadville, Pennsylvania. My father had gone there many years before. In spite of that I had never seen or heard about the place. I was simply taken to the Winnetka train station, and handed a train ticket. Mother said good by. Arrival at Meadville was all alone, and was a special point in my life. I had to find the college. I had no real problem, but it was extremely lonely.

The college was good about explaining where I was to stay, and about classes. First I had to take lots of tests. The tests were to determine how intelligent or dumb each student was. Well I passed the medical aptitude test with the best grades ever, but English construction test was a pitiful flop.

Before classes started the college had a party for all new students. This was at a camp in the woods near Meadville. Here new boys met new girls. Ah, now I was in my element! Right off I met Nancy Greener who lived in town. Soon we were dating regularly and she was a wonderful person in every way.

It turned out that Nancy's father was a professor in the physics department. Eventually I took one of his classes and his family took me to their hearts and fed me many excellent home cooked dinners. Nancy and I became very close and after a couple of years I asked her to marry me, and she agreed. Mostly I dreamed of having children with Nancy.

However, my parents were dead set against marriage for me and they pressured me severely to give up my crazy thoughts about marriage. The pressure was the kind that could only come from the head of 10,000 screaming political activists. Mother was a very controlling person. But also my parents had never before had the experience of one of their children getting married.

At Meadville I was spending most of my time outside of the college working. Well to be honest, all my time I didn't spend with Nancy I was working. Home work was a very secondary consideration. I worked for a TV repair shop putting up antennas and repairing radios. The work was dangerous and risky. In those days we would put up a 20 foot piece of pipe on the top of each house with a TV antenna on the top. Guy wires to the four corners of the roof held the mast.

The trouble with this was that houses in this area were two and three stories tall, a century old, and had mossy slate roofs. Somehow I avoided slipping on the moss and falling into the streets. But the work paid well and I had enough money to eat and live reasonably well at the college. Most important was that I had money to date Nancy. But the work also gave me my first experience with spy work.

My boss had heard that a town near by had "cable television". This was something new as he said there were only three cable systems in the world. Cable TV looked like a real hot item, and of course in time it proved to be true. He gave me his car and plenty of money to go and find out the technical details about how to build a "cable TV" system.

In those days only big bars and rich people could afford "cable TV". So I visited lots of "speak easy" style bars, as those were the only type in that rough and tough Polish coal mining area. The risks were high but I cruised up and down the streets looking at the "cable" and spent lots of time talking to anyone I could find knowledgeable about "The Cable". I reported everything necessary to build a cable TV system to my boss.

After two years of college my engagement to Nancy was off, my college career was finished due to lack of studying, but my first industrial spy job was quite a success. It was a low spot in my life.

7

SHIPS OFFICER

Back at New Hall High School a number of us took several courses in radio under a good teacher "J. C." Palmer. We all joined the same radio club too and became close friends. "J. C." taught a one full year course in electronic theory and Morse code. The second year he also taught a commercial radio course and the requirement was to obtain your Federal Communications Commission "Radio Telephone First Class" and "Radio Telegraph Second Class" licenses. These would allow a person to obtain work at a radio station, or on a U.S. Merchant Marine ship. Well I got all the licenses with as high a ranking as I could obtain without actual time at sea.

When my love affair with Nancy Greener collapsed in a shambles, and my college grades were awful, the FCC licenses turned out to be a real God send. Because I had these licenses I was able to get a job at station WQR in Evanston, Illinois. Work was about 96 hours a week. I shoveled the snow, pumped up the leaky coax transmission line, logged the transmitter, chose all the music, was a full time disk jockey, and simultaneously recorded all the programs for times when I just had to sleep.

Living the life of a "slave" was more that I could stand. In addition the pay was bad, there is no other way to express it! On paper I was paid a good deal and this fake amount was reported to the Internal Revenue Service as expenses by the owner. He then paid the tax on my alleged salary and kept the difference. Pretty tricky book keeping, but that seems to be how radio and TV stations are run. Well that job went walking after a few months.

Later I took a job as an electronic technician for a company manufacturing test equipment. This company would buy up surplus electronic components and repackage them as new. We filled the containers with small rocks chips swept up from the roads and filled the empty parts of the packages with road tar so they would not rattle. The downfall was when the top fell off one of the units because the owner was to cheap to even buy rivets and the military inspector was greeted with a lap full of crushed rock. Well one more job down the tubes.

All the time I was learning about the real world. With the electronics company I also learned more about industrial espionage. There are a lot of tricks that make the job easier. The one, two, three, of it is this way: Go look and see what has been published on the subject at hand. Often the people you want to steal from are just dying to send you all sorts of printed information, particularly if you say you are going to buy their "thing". Two, if easy "research" does not provide enough information then go and talk to people who work at the company. Be a good buddy to them, buy them drinks. Ask leeding questions. Remember that old Latin saying about "in wine there is truth". Third, if all else fails then penetrate the company by getting a job there and learning (stealing) all you can. International spy work is exactly the same. Actually only the third step is dangerous.

Back in High School I had spent much time with Chad Haney (now Dr. Chad Haney). I was the radio electronics expert and local explosives expert too (actuallyI got my information from Encyclopedia Britanica). I spent a lot of time at his house and together with the police chief's son, Rodger Haines, we blew up his mothers flower garden, terrorized the neighborhood, and generally had good times.

Chad introduced me to a former president of Czechoslovakia Edvard Reisz and his family. They were running from the KGB at the time and we spent some time in their hideout in the Wisconsin woods. As I remember the living room of the hideout had a circular gun rack in the middle and little else. For fun we threw hand grenades off a cliff in the woods nearby. When not otherwise occupied I would spend my time talking with Mr. Reisz and his daughter who was my age. Mr. Reisz had wonderful stories in a mix of German, English, and Latin, about meeting Adolf Hitler and Joseph Steelman, about riding long ago with the White Communist Russian cavalry in Siberia. He told me how to feed my horse fermented horse milk called kumis, and then jump on and ride another 20 kilometers. His daughter in addition had terrible but fascinating stories about what the Communist Russian soldiers did to her. This meeting with the famous Reisz family was important later on in my life.

At a critical moment in my life Chad Haney came to rescue me and said that his father knew of a couple of radio officer jobs on a passenger ship and would I like to try it? I am afraid that they had do a little convincing in my case, but luckily they were good salesmen. So both Chad and I shipped out on the steam passenger ship S.S. North American as radio officers.

First I had to get special security clearance as the Great Lakes were critical to iron production in the United States. No one could pass through the Sault St. Marie American locks into Lake Superior without such a clearance. All sailors were under suspicion in the days of Joseph McCarthy's communist witch hunts as he claimed all sailors were supposed to belong to communist organizations. Then there were all the various Coast Guard papers. I somehow also became a Purser, Coal Passer, Seaman, and Radio Officer too. Best of all was the special uniform that we had to wear on the passenger ship. A blue naval officers uniform with a single gold stripe on the sleeve was considered necessary. Lastly was a white officer's hat with black, red, and gold flag insignia.

Remarkably this hat insignia was the German post World War II flag. Probably it was because the company was German owned and the smoke stacks were also painted in the German colors. We didn't speculate on that much.

We had lots of special cruises to ports in Wisconsin, and the ship was filled with frolicking Wisconsin Germans. I learned that beer was the drink of choice, and that raw hamburger mixed with raw onion was the food of choice. On occasion we would disgorge these drunk Wisconsinites on some unsuspecting town. The results were generally that the fire and police departments were taken over by drunken passengers. Fire trucks would parade up and down the streets with sirens going, followed by the town's police cars. Everything was "gutmutligkeit" (good times). I'll bet the ordinary people were glad to hear our whistle blow to recall the passengers to the ship... of course we always lost a few passengers at such a stop because they were too drunk to hear the whistle.

Another kind of cruise was made for serious gamblers. There were just a few people that could afford this kind of a cruise. The few aficionados would board in Chicago followed by a Douglas Armored Car. The armoreded car drivers would fill a state room with cash and stay with it 24 hours a day. All poker games were played with strictly cash and I have seen as much as $50,000. dollars in the pot at a time. Our players never ate much, and drank even less. A sandwich and a glass of whiskey was the standard fare. The whiskey was only used to wet the lips which never smiled. This was dead serious gambling with big pots of real cash.

Ordinary cruises were made from places like Chicago, Detroit, Buffalo, Cleveland, Mackinac Island, Midland Ontario, and back to Chicago. The ship was full of people just enjoying themselves eating, drinking, talking, and often enjoying sex.

I remember a couple of boastful men brought a "lady of easy virtue" on board. They extravagantly boasted to me of all the sex they were going to have for a week. Their stateroom was right below the Radio Shack on our ship. I can vouch for the fact that they each had sex for a couple of hours on the first day of the cruise. After that the "lady" just enjoyed her view for the remainder of the week!

For the unmarried ship's officers there was a tremendous amount of play interspersed with work. After my wild life at Angeles College I fit right in.

We also had other crew on the steamer. There were bell boys, galley cooks, waitresses, seamen, and more. The seamen were all from Sicily, a tough wiry bunch who knew their trade inside and out. These seaman were a quiet bunch who seldom went ashore. They spent their spare time knitting and working knots. They made everything they could, to make their floating home comfortable, and wisely saved their money.

At one time I walked into the galley and found two Polish cooks fighting it out with long butcher knives. They were facing each other and slashing, screaming in Polish all the time. I avoided getting between them as it looked like lethal combat. I went out and called the Sicilian sailors and told them the problem. Shortly both Polish cooks were gone, never to reappear on our ship. I didn't ask what happened!

Now as for the waitresses, they really held my interest! It was suggested by the Captain that I should start a ship's news paper along with a particularly good looking, tall, thin, woman named Jan Klein from Brownsburg, Illinois. She sold the newspaper's advertising at our various ports, and also helped write the paper. I got the news off the radio and helped write parts of the paper too. I would type it all up and mimeograph copies to distribute to the passengers. Jan would sell them to the passengers with a smile, and to the men perhaps with a suggestion of something more! She was infamous among the crew for her "salesmanship". I accompanied her ashore often. But in those days one girl was not enough and I was living in what I must term "Fat City"...

One amusing story is that I felt very tired and run down. I went to the ship's doctor and asked what was wrong. He took a good long look at me, and said nothing for a long time. Then he said "lay off the girls!". I said, "Doc how did you know?". His answer was "Well you have lipstick on your uniform collar!". And you know he was right. I started living a very slightly more monastic life and I did feel better!

The only trouble with this passenger ship job was that the ship quit running in the winter. This is only natural since in September it was beginning to turn cold on the Great Lakes. So I decided to go back to my studies at a new college. This time I decided to go to Lake Washington University in Lake Forest, Illinois.

Here I took a full load of courses, including Spanish. I did much better in classes than at Angeles and I did not work full time at other jobs. My only non-scholastic enjoyment was a buddy who was also interested in explosives to a much greater degree than me. He was pretty good at it too, and knew almost every chemical formula for explosives I had ever read in books. Moreover he had made a Mason jar sized sample of almost all of them and had them stored in the basement of his parents home.

However, my friend did make a few errors. One was putting a very sensitive explosive on the dormitory toilet seat bumpers. One day a husky foot ball player sat on one of his booby trapped toilets.

He immediately knew my friend was responsible and beat the tar out of him. Later on he blew the porch off the dorm, and blew up the lab where he was doing summer work. Neither explosion was ever explained. Well he is now a respected PhD in chemistry and would probably like to forget his past.

I was still living at home and I felt my mother always seemed to be "on my case" and allowed me no leeway. I was paying all my education fees and everything else, but she still was trying to manipulate my life, no doubt with the very best intent. At least that was my feeling.

One day my friend at the college invited me on a double date with him. We ended up spending the night at his girl friend's house in the farm country north west of Chicago. I got to take the younger sister as my date. She appeared to be 18 to my eyes. Indeed the local bar apparently thought so too. Before turning in for the night my date let me have the astounding news that "I am 15 years old, well maybe 14... but it will only be a month until I am 15". Wow! The result was that I spent the night in a rather monastic fashion with a 14 year old virgin. And she was still a virgin in the morning!

Somehow my date got the idea I should marry her, and right now too! Between this farm girl and my mother's manipulations I decided that it was time to pull up my tent pegs and move to Mexico, quick. I would load up my "Hog" Harley-Davidson motorcycle with essentials and hit the road. I could even visit with my Friend Emma down in Missouri along the way. Well at 23 years old I could get a chance to use some of that Spanish I had been learning, and I could see where my mother's family had lived so long ago.

ALONE IN THE JUNGLE

I THINK IT WAS January 1953 that I started my trip to Mexico. It was cold riding a "hog" in Illinois in mid winter and I looked forward to some good warm weather somewhere to the south. I left a note in my Winnetka bedroom saying that I was going to see Friend Emma and nothing more.

All my cash had been pulled out of my bank account and I took off with no notice to anyone. Seemed safer that way. The trip through the flat farm land of Illinois was not very interesting. When I came to southern Illinois I found the people spoke a different dialect of English. My motor cycle became a "sickle", and it took me a while to figure out what people were saying.

When I got to Missouri I remember meeting with Friend Emma in some nondescript eating joint. When we were young we wrote each other what I thought at the time were some pretty passionate letters. Now she was in deeply in love with a fellow named Maxwell who she said was rich and the scion of a well to do family from Quincy, Illinois. She was going to marry him as I remember and didn't want to be seen with me. The meeting was awful and pointless and I was glad to be on my way south again.

That night it was darn cold I remember. All alone I pulled into a remote dirt road that went out into the woods. This was my first experience with motorcycle camping and I was freezing. I built a small fire and heated a few small boulders. I kept these under my blankets indian fashion to keep from freezing. In spite of being awake half the night I felt refreshed and ready to ride when the sun came up over the hill.

Another night I pulled into a small camp ground that looked like a good place to rest. I was wrong! It was occupied by a mountain lion going through the trash barrel. Not liking what was showing in my head light I told the lion "You can have this place, it is all yours!".

At last I arrived at the Border and crossed over with no problems. A few miles past the border there was a military road block. I was stopped by one of the troops with a very long 1898 Mauser rifle. He wanted to see my "papers". I pulled out my merchant marine papers and said in English that I was a "marine" which remarkably impressed him. The marines who invaded Mexico in the past had really left their mark! Anyway, I was passed through the check point pretty damn quick.

In those days roads in Mexico were not marked on the map. At one place just south of the Texas border I remember following donkey trails for mile after mile. There was little other traffic except for an occasional bus bouncing along dirt roads that appeared to be nothing more than random tire tracks.

One place I followed a bad set of tire tracks weaving through the cactus for many miles until I came to a canyon. Apparently there was some difference of opinion between the road builder and the bridge contractor. The bridge across the canyon was perhaps a kilometer down stream from the road, and it had a barricade across my end. To get across the river one had to take a narrow road down the side of a cliff to the canyon floor and then pay to take a ferry across the river. I figured probably the bridge builder was the ferry boat captains brother, and he didn't want him to lose any business.

The solution of the ferry boat problem on a motorcycle was easy. I just rode down a horse trail to the bridge. There was plenty of room for a horse, or a motorcycle, to bypass the barricade, so that is just what I did. No toll either!

Riding on down the road near Tampico it is swamp on either side of the road, no detours. Going through this desolate swamp I ran across two policemen blocking the road with their bodies. Both were enjoying a good marijuana smoke. You know, that burning grass smell. As nearly as I could translate one of the policemen wanted my motorcycle. I told him it was all I had, and I wouldn't give it up. Well his hand slid down to the butt of his pistol, and suddenly my mind changed. He took the motorcycle and disappeared. I asked the remaining policeman where he went, but the marijuana had him feeling so cool he just didn't want to talk. Was the machine gone forever, or what?

I sat at the side of the road for several hours trying to figure what to do next. Suddenly in the distance I could see my "hog" coming back down the road. The policeman pulled up and profusely thanked me for the ride. We were all buddies now! He had taken the machine over to his village and ridden up and down the street to show his neighbors that he really could ride a motorcycle, just like he had learned in the Army, and just like he had told them!

Another day in Ciudad Valles I was threading my way through trucks, burros, horses, and pedestrians. Many people were shouting in Spanish "The Red is dead. The Red is dead." This was completely beyond my comprehension. I had to stop and ask what was going on. The answer from a pedestrian was "Steelman has died!". This was a truly momentous thing in Mexico where communists had a tremendous popular interest between about 1900 and 1917. It was an almost communist type revolt of the peasants. It happened just before the Communist Russians had begun their revolution. There was much trading of ideas between Mexico and Russia in those days so Steelman was well known in Mexico.

In fact I remembered my Grandfather talking of meeting important Communist Russians in Mexico during "The Mexican Revolution". It was his job as promoter to try to meet anyone who might need his services. So he never missed a chance to greet someone famous, or infamous. However, I had no such tendencies at the time.

Mostly my problem was to save money and stay alive. I ate mostly beans as they were about seventeen cents a day. For trail food I carried oranges and bananas in my saddle bags. Sometimes I would get some sugar or Mexican chocolate too. You should know that real Mexican chocolate has about ten times the stimulating effect of a cup of coffee. It is full of theobromin, which is very much like super caffeine. On occasion I might run across one of the very excellent Mexican bakeries and get some really decadent food.

Much of my time was outside of cities living all alone. It gave me plenty of time to reflect on things like the exceptionally bad slash and burn farming practices I could see. There would be a line of slash and burn farms with a jungle on one side and a desert on the other. No one had taught the Indians in many areas how to conserve the scarce mountain farm land. Three or four years of this kind of agriculture would turn the land into desert.

On the other hand I found superlative and massive Indian building projects in the mountains. In places there were stone walls that stretched for miles. These ran over hills, mountains, and valleys. They were made from non standard sized stones all fit together so perfectly that concrete was never required. The same was true of massive ceremonial platforms on the sides of steep mountains. They had endured for centuries without upkeep and were works of stone art.

Unlike normal tourists I spent my time on the land and in the country side. There I found that the farmers got up at perhaps four A.M. in the morning and started for their fields. By the first light they would be working on their crops. A little after noon they had put in a full day working in the cool of the morning. No lazy people here.

I often slept in crop fields as they were more comfortable. I tried to do this out of sight as much as possible to avoid problems. But it didn't always work out. It was dark and I was sleeping soundly in a recently plowed field when I felt a sharp jab. Two Indians were sticking me with very lethal needle sharp spears. They had me cold, and in the moon light they wanted to know what I was doing in their field.

Boy was I thinking fast! I told them in Spanish that "not all North Americans are rich and some have to sleep in the fields." This seemed to really do the trick, they liked my story! So I went on to say "Your blankets are much better than mine!". With this they lowered their spears and came over to inspect my blankets by feel. Then they felt their home spun serapes, the difference in quality was tremendous. They laughed and disappeared. Saved!

The next morning a truck passed with a couple of men riding in the back. They yelled at me in Spanish "Hey, poor boy!". I knew these were my spear holders of the night before.

You have always got to be willing to think and act when faced with adversity. That was the lesson I learned on the motorcycle trail. It sure helps to speak the language of the country you are in too. But being willing to give in a little is important too.

Another night alone in the jungle I pulled into a place to sleep. The ground looked comfortable. I could see in the moon light the place was surrounded by good sized sticks which I started tossing back to make a place for my blankets. I went to pick up one stick and found it was really a snake as big as my arm! Well again I said "Snake you can have this place. It is all yours!". As for sleeping in the fields and jungles, yes occasionally there are problems.

After a while it looked like my money was running low and I started looking for work. Mexican pay was terrible. In addition I was a foreigner without proper papers. I heard from people that there was good work north of the border, but then everyone seemed to know about that. I headed for Texas.

Arriving at the border somehow I heard of a company in Houston that was looking for people with electronic ship board experience. I was immediately hired and sent to their office in Louisiana. Here I was to learn to navigate ships in the Gulf of Mexico. What a change. But I had no idea of how much of a change this was going to be.

LIFE AT SEA AND SIMILAR TALES

Arriving at Morgan City, Louisiana in the middle of the Cajun country was a real change for me. Everyone at my office spoke English, and that was a change too. My new boss was Bob Puchaty recently from the coal fields of Pennsylvania. He started me out sweeping the office floor. I think it was a test just to see if I would do it without grumbling. Then he assigned me to an offshore seismic exploration vessel. I would learn how to navigate under an Indian man named Charles Bigman. My teacher was from Oklahoma; he commonly went by the name of "Pony", perhaps because he was small.

"Pony" was a really tough, excellent, teacher and believed in all work and no play, everything was dead serious. We spent about a month on the ship doing navigation side by side until I had sufficiently learned the trade. We worked from before sun up until after sun down every day for ten days at a time. We would attempt to navigate the ship's mid point to within fifteen feet of a new, but invisible, point in the water of the Gulf every five minutes. Then we stopped and fifty pounds of high explosive was tossed overboard from a another ship four hundred feet astern and exploded. This resulted in a geyser several hundred feet in the air. The blast would hit our ship like an iron fist. A sonic echo from the explosion would tell if there was oil below us.

My assigned bunk on the ship was right under an air vent leeding in from the upper deck. It had rusted in place so that it was like a funnel facing directly toward the oncoming ocean waves. When the weather was rough the waves would hit the funnel and dump buckets of water on my bunk. This made it necessary to sleep in full rain gear. My bed was constantly wet.

The psychology of the crew was intriguing. We had one of our crew who spent most of his time bragging about his time in the Marines. To hear him tell it he was the roughest, and the toughest, of the toughest. Death didn't bother him a bit. He could withstand anything, no punishment was beyond his guts. Except when one day when we had fifteen foot waves crashing over the bow he began to scream "We're sinking, we're sinking!!!! We're all going to die!!!!". In addition he curled up in fetal position on his bunk while screaming. We "old salts" had a good laugh. But our ship also had a lot of other real dangerous psychological problems.

There were thirteen men on a 55 foot diesel powered boat. This means that we were packed in fairly tight, almost shoulder to shoulder. After a ten day stint at sea the tensions were always tight as a tick full of blood. I expected a murder at any time. Of course at sea it would easy.

Ship board radio communications were also my job along with updating precision navigation fixes every minute. One day I heard the following startling radio conversation: "Hey John, Pete just fell overboard." The answer I heard was: "You getting any fish?" Again the first boat answered, "Yeah we're getting fish." John answered back with the astounding words "Forget him!" Clearly life at sea was not worth much!

I spent three months on this ship as a single navigator. We were captained by a man the crew universally called "Billy Bly" for good reason. He was out to prove to his company he could do more "work" in ten days than any other ship. He did this by making his "shots" at one half the distance of any other ship and hoped to do them all in the same time. His math was faulty since we had to stop and restart the ship for each shot point. All required time. In addition it was necessary to accelerate from each stop from zero speed to about 14 knots, a non-linear function. The result was that the ship was averaging a less than normal forward average speed. It also took me vastly more time to compensate for those existing ocean side currents which sometimes were a lot faster than our average forward speed.

"Billy Bly" brooked no excuses for any reason, even if it was the laws of the Universe. His own lack of math skills was a thing he simply did not admit, or perhaps he did not want to understand. He had told his boss ashore that he was going to get twice the production of any other ships, math laws be damned. I suspect I told him he was an idiot, but I simply don't remember. At any rate I was his scape goat when he did not achieve all he bragged he could do. In consequence I went ashore to a new job. You might say I was fired.

I was replaced by two navigators, and never again did my own company try to use a single man on such a strenuous 18 hour a day job where the tension was exceedingly high. Luckily my company had a new job for me.

I became the roving engineer for their networks of shore stations and now and then navigator on various other ships. One ship was the company's own research vessel the MV Hyperac. Tensions were never high on this ship and it was an extremely pleasant change.

From time to time I worked with Knut Anker-Goli. Knut was a relaxed Norwegian who was navigator on a more easy-going ship. Indeed Knut had fixed up a couch in the back of the pilot house where he could lay back and watch his instruments which he had screwed to the ceiling. Frankly I think only certain women can make an income on their backs. I had to hand it to Knut to figure how to manage it too.

Another unusual thing happened on shore. A well educated university professor came to our office wanting work, on a ship, and he wanted it "right now, and for several months". He was pursued by a sheriff and a very pregnant woman who arrived at the office just after he left for his new ship job.

We all had to wait several months to hear the outcome of the "romance", but what an unbelievable story. The Professor claimed he was forced into sex by lots of women. My sarcastic thought was "that's a likely story".

When we went to the local restaurant for lunch with the Professor who was dressed in nothing but a sweaty tee shirt and jeans, the three of us were treated to an unbelievable thing. After a few minutes sitting several women just drifted over to our table and threw themselves at the Professor. Just like he said it was! It was this way every time I had lunch with the Professor too. He had what they called "animal magnetism" in the old days. Today I think it would be said he had an excess of "sex pheromones", the natural chemical odor you can't smell but that thing that affects relationships. It was my first experience with "pheromones", but there was to be another almost identical episode in Fairbanks, Alaska years later.

The Hyperac shore stations were located in very remote parts of the Louisiana Cajun swamps. I developed special electronic methods to keep them on the air much more reliably, and in addition I generally maintained the stations and their associated communications equipment. The regular station operators were given four days off each two weeks. I would take over as a roving engineer. Consequently I sold my motorcycle and bought a used telephone company panel truck.

This van had room for a cot in the back, also some food shelves, and some room for radio amateur equipment. Now I could visit the different shore stations in pure comfort. During my time off I would also take the truck to New Orleans to swim in Lake Ponchatrain. It was a great improvement in my life style, which basically remained monastic.

Due to radio propagation problems at sun rise and sun set, the company decided not to run their radio stations at night. A couple of us were radio hams and we saw a great opportunity in this as the existing antennas were almost exactly tuned for the 160 meter ham frequencies. All we had to do was attach a transmitter and we did. We loved the tremendous results that were produced by a 150 foot tall top loaded vertical antenna and the 120 ground radials that spread out around the base.

Jack Hammer and I were able to talk all over the United States with ease on the 160 meter ham band. The only trouble was that we two unknowingly became an international incident. In Canada the Mounties used the same frequencies, and we unknowingly blotted them out. The Federal Communications Commission solved the problem by making it illegal for any Louisiana radio amateur to operate on the 160 meter ham band. A rather Draconian solution, but what else could be expected from Washington.

After a while The Company moved me over to Cameron, deep in the coastal salt water swamps of western Louisiana. There I had thirteen ships under my aegis. There were two types of vessels, seismic exploration ships with electronic instruments, and shooting boats loaded to the gills with high explosives. There were continual large and small problems to solve each day. I also had three shore Hyperac navigation stations to look after. Our problems were certainly interesting.

On one ship the operator complained "My nav receiver isn't working so well after we were hit by lightning!" Well when they came into dock I found that they indeed had been hit by a lightning bolt and their nine foot antenna was melted down to a six inch long ball of slag. Remarkably there was no other damage to the rugged equipment.

Another ship complained that their communications "weren't worth a diddley". I asked when this problem started. The operator told me it was right after he and the cook had a bottle of wine at the mess table one night and then decided to "fix" their communications antenna to look just like the shrimp boat antennas that were passing by. To do this they simply cut off most of our very critically tuned antenna, with no readjustment to compensate for the amputation. The antenna was indeed now totally worthless. I had to agree with their assessment!

One day I heard a call on the communications radio "the ship is on fire!!!" This was one of "my" boats, so I listened very closely as I knew it was loaded to the gunnels with tons of explosives. In a little while the voice said "we're leaving the ship." They rowed over to another ship which then pulled away perhaps ten miles. All day they watched their ship slowly smoulder. At long last I heard "The skipper has decided we should go back and put the fire out." They started back when I suddenly heard the startled words "The ship exploded!!!" There was nothing left but a mushroom cloud and a lot of unnerved seamen who had almost got on board the doomed vessel.

The men were all given two weeks paid vacation to pull themselves together again. Most of the men told me they were going to quit the sea forever. Actually all returned to the sea after two weeks leave ashore.

Another time I had a call from one of our navigators that a plane had crashed in the sea near him. It was an Air Force B-52 bomber, one of a group on an atomic bomb world covering exercise. We mobilized our communications network and all of our available ships in the area to look for the Air Force crew and plane. We also got the Air Force to shift their transmitters over to our special frequencies so everyone could assist in the search. Several days of our time were spent without results and sadly the crew was lost. Nonetheless, we did have exact coordinates where the plane had crashed and helped the Air Force to recover things from the ocean bottom, what I presumed was an atomic bomb.

For some reason I was becoming well known back at the main company office at Tulsa, Oklahoma. One day they called me up and asked me if I would like to try out some secret overseas work they were doing for the United States. I said sure.

I had asked Pony about this kind of work and I found out my company essentially sold your body to DoD to do what ever DoD need done. Things that they could not do, or things they did not think they should be visibly doing themselves. Most of the work would be special ship navigation, but there could be many other things too. And he mentioned that we would have to wear uniforms with insignia too. I guess I still had good memories of the uniform I wore on the Great Lakes passenger ships. It all sounded great to me, and there was a raise involved too.

10

PART TIME SOLDIER OF FORTUNE

THE WORLD WAS changing fast in those days. There was the Cold War which was very hot for some of us. There had been the Korean War too. There was communist intrigue on a world wide scale never known before. It was the days of the semi fictional British Agent Kurt Strong. Perhaps a certain amount of Agent 007 was based on real happenings, who knows...

Certainly my life was changing in a radical fashion. I was to become what is often called a "soldier of fortune", sort of a hired gun. Yes I was to work for DoD, and yes I was to wear a uniform according to their rule book. But no I was not to even think about wearing any insignia of any kind, even if the rule book says so. Yes I was to have the equivalent rank of Navy Captain if I was working for the Navy, and Colonel if I was working for the Army. My secret rank was to always be telegraphed ahead in coded secret messages.

One of my first military projects was to set up a radio navigation station on a small island near the Turks and Cacios Island group. Like an invading army we came to within about five miles of the island in a LST (Landing Ship Tank). At this point we lowered the large ramp at the bow of the ship and drove amphibious landing craft off into the ocean. Each of the craft was like a cross between a boat and a truck, they had wheels and a propeller too. Out in the ocean they were very low in the water and almost invisible from land. However I believe a good wave could sink us instantly.

We charged up on a beach at the foot of a cliff. The beach was all jagged coral which would cut tires and shoes, but for some reason it was the place we had been commanded to go ashore. Only sea gulls opposed our landing.

At this point we set up a navigation beacon and a communications radio station. Out at sea they were laying out special submarine detection devices to find Communist Russian submarines operating below the temperature inversion layer where surface ships could not detect them.

The Russians had been very interested in this operation as the United States was testing some of our latest military technology. They had sent some of their spies over to study what was being done. Being at remote location perhaps we did not get the best quality of the Communist Russian spies, and they were plenty obvious. They were discovered right away by the British Intelligence MI6 people, and "their" work was "terminated", according to my discussions with MI6.

Having the rank of Captain was wonderful as I was commonly equal to the actual captain of the ship. Often this meant that we dined together on the ship and at least I always secured a special seat in the officer's mess. I was able to meet some very interesting people this way as we cruised the world. It also meant that by Navy protocol I had to "buy into the officer's mess" of each ship. The officers of each ship purchased their own food and operated according to their own private rules and billing procedures. Since I sailed on a lot of ships, I spent several years sorting out all the different bills from each officer's mess.

While I was involved in this kind of work my military draft number came up. I went to Chicago and took the physical exam. In spite of the fact that I had vision in only one eye they still wanted to draft me. This was war time and anyone who could walk and talk was drafted. For me they proposed a special position as a private soldier running a military entertainment radio station.

When my friends at the Department of Defense (DoD) heard about this they said "We'll fix that!". They wrote an official letter to my Draft Board saying that I was already completely involved with the military and was essential to the Nation's security. I never again heard a word from my Draft Board. Frankly I liked being a high ranking officer and would have chaffed badly as a common private.

My military projects were sometimes ashore, and sometimes at sea, or in the air. There was a wide range of projects and they became more complex as time went by. In my early days with DoD I did a lot of shore station projects in a wide range of locations. These were interspersed with navigation of a number of different types of ships used for a number of purposes. Some vessels were 450 feet long with masses of people and complex electronics. Other craft were only 50 feet long and disguised as fishing boats. Then again some were perhaps 200 feet long, top heavy with electronics and so very narrow so that they rolled alarmingly. At one time I even navigated a massive cable laying ship. Another time a salvage vessel picking up secret scientific equipment from 2000 fathoms down on the bottom of the "Bermuda Triangle" before the Communist Russians could get it. Other times it was living on a remote island with Africans who had never seen white people before. There was unquestionably plenty of variety.

At certain point I began navigation of helicopters, and eventually I became a helicopter pilot. We had many different missions in helicopters and all seemed to be unusual. At one time my experience with high explosives became known and I instantly became a helicopter navigator and bombardier. As our chopper was taking off from the stern of a ship someone would run out and put a bomb in my lap. I would then hold it until I had navigated to the exact coordinates commanded. At that point I would make sure we were high enough we wouldn't get blasted out of the air by our own bomb and throw it overboard. How much fun can a young guy have?

Some places I had lots of explosives to play with. I couldn't resist doing a few private experiments. For example I experimented to see how many fish and what sorts of fish would succumb to a pretty good bomb blast. We had killed fish by the thousands in the Gulf of Mexico accidentally. With my diving equipment I very carefully I selected a spot in a reef with plenty of fish of a wide variety and let the blast go. The results were totally unexpected in many ways.

First was the fact that about ninety percent of the fish were apparently unaffected by the blast and simply disappeared from the area. Of the fish actually killed only about ten percent floated to the surface, and ninety percent sank to the bottom. I concluded that "DuPont spinners" as some people called them were clearly not an efficient way to fish and I never again tried that method of fish experiments. But there were other results.

When I got back to the secret base where I was working I heard about the fantastic undersea avalanche that had happened that day. It was the talk of the day among the military people looking for Communist Russian submarines. I never did tell them that it was really my fishing experiment that just sounded like an avalanche.

When I was not working on some secret project I would work at my company's research laboratory at Tulsa, Oklahoma. I was a part time soldier of fortune and part time researcher. There were plenty of fun projects in the lab too. They fairly well let me do what I wanted to do with just a little direction from my Tulsa boss Bob Penny.

One project was to develop a computer to find faults in the radio navigation transmitters. In those days there were no small computers but I did understand computer Boolean mathematical concepts. My result was a computer made with electrical relays having "and", "or", and "flip-flop" functions. It worked beautifully, and I patented it and several other inventions. In reality it was so far ahead of the technicians that no one could understand it, thus rendering it effectively unusable.

Those were the early days of "credit cards". Not everyone carried one, or a dozen. In our business we were issued unlimited international air travel cards. In other words we could fly anywhere in the world any time we wanted. Occasionally this lead to some people taking world tours. As for me, I tried to be very careful in how I used my blank checks.

My assignments often came to me in a strange ways. I would find an unsigned note on my office desk saying something like "Go to Trinidad today and meet Peter in the International Bar". I would grab my already packed bag and run for the airport. With unlimited travel money there would always be an airline and a route to get where I needed to be.

Many of my destinations were in the islands of the Caribbean. One place was Barbados, today an independent country. In those days there were almost no tourists. Air travel in those days was entirely by

Enigma Overseas Airways Company or EOAC. My British friends said that stood for "Easy Outwitting A Camel".

To go to Barbados I would fly to Puerto Rico on an American airline and change over to EOAC. We then would island hop down through the Antilles via former World War II airports built to send B17 bombers to Europe. In those days the bombers would fly from island to island then across to Africa and then up to England. In more recent days we would land at each small airport and be served complementary and powerful rum punch drinks. Without tremendous amount of caution a person could easily get totally smashed on such a trip.

My first job in Barbados was totally non electronic, it was to prepare the people of the island for an immanent friendly invasion of U.S. Navy people. This worked out reasonably well. On the appointed day many large Navy ships anchored in the harbor and small boats filled with men started ashore. The official Barbados uniformed band went down to the dock along with thousands of island residents. As the boats came ashore the band struck up "Le Marseilles" and played it over and over. Some how I had missed the mark, and they thought this was the French navy coming ashore, or perhaps they only had one sheet of music.

On another trip I arrived and visited the U.S. Embassy to ask what I was supposed to be doing on the island. The answer was startling, and just what every red blooded guy full of hormones dreams of hearing. "Your job is to 'entertain' the daughters of government officials here… we'll make the dates for you." I had a small British automobile and was living in old Colonial style hotel. All I had to do was pick up the girls and take them to night clubs where we would dance and have a drink or two, or what ever they desired!

Again it was "Fat City" time! I met an number of very nice girls and certainly learned a lot about the governments on all the adjacent islands. One was the daughter of a Prime Minister of an Island Nation. She was a wonderful and intelligent girl. I'll admit it was a bit of a physical strain running around every night, sort of like being on the S.S. North American. But at least I found out exactly what Kurt Strong's life was really like!

For a while I even lived at a light house on the north end of the Island of Barbados. It was a wonderful time for me living on top of a windy cliff overlooking the Atlantic. Once I was invited to a near by sugar cane plantation. The house was built about 1700 and furnished with things brought from China by clipper ship. The same family had been in attendance since it was built. It was like going back two hundred years and the hospitality was equivalent.

One day a raft washed up on the rock near the light house. Aboard was a Frenchman who seemed at death's door, and in truth he actually was dying. He had cancer and had decided he would do one last great thing in his life, he would sail the Atlantic Ocean, alone on a piece of plywood. He was equipped with only a tarp to obtain rain water for drinking and a very fine fish net to scoop up plankton for food along the way. With real, first class, French élan, he completed the trip alone, and died a few days later.

Another time I swam out to a small catamaran that had just sailed across the Atlantic Ocean with two German brothers. They were steel workers and had welded up two canoe like hulls, each just large enough to sleep one person plus holding some food supplies. The deck was about an eight by eight foot square of flat metal. They had a board with a nail driven through for their only navigation instrument. Each day they would measure the length of the nail's shadow at local noon to determine their latitude. It worked and they managed to cross the ocean.

When on the very remote island of Barbuda I had a curious experience. I felt a 'presence' behind me and found a white man just standing there. Since I knew I was the only white man near by, I asked where he came from. His answer was a laconic "from a boat". I wanted to know "what boat and where?" His response was something like "my sail boat is The Transworld and my name is Chris England". He went on to say "I just sailed alone across the Atlantic Ocean, and I've got a B19 Mark II radio on board, can you help me make it work?" It was a World War II British tank radio, and I just happened to know it well, and we did make it work. Years later a popular book was written about Chris England and his remarkable solo world trips, but I was his first contact.

At one time I was put ashore on an island inhabited only by black Africans. The last white person they had seen was during World War I according to their leader. I got to live in a tent close to their village of thatched huts. Life was very different for these people, but I was the big attraction for the moment. At dawn every day they would open the flaps on my tent and watch my every movement silently. Dozens would follow me as I went out in the bush to have a morning pee, or what ever. There was no way to say go away since we did not speak a common language and sign language was ignored. At least I learned how not to be embarrassed any more. There is nothing quite like having a couple of dozen people watch you defecate to take the edge off any those civilized concepts of nudity that one had been trained to respect since childhood.

Another time I was "lucky" enough to spend a night in one of the local thatched huts. Inside I slept on the clean mud floor, but the place had dozens of lizards and other things crawling about in the thatch of the roof, and even more fleas found their dinner at my side. Frankly it took me two weeks to get rid of the horrible fleas and their bites.

These experiences I had with remarkable lone sailors of the great Atlantic Ocean, making their solo trips, in very minimal boats, made me believe that certainly the Norwegians, or the Irish, or perhaps Indians or Eskimos, could have done the same thing. In the Pacific Ocean certainly primitive people sailed long distances in the various types of boats they had available even thousand's of years ago. It certainly was not necessary to wait for a theoretical "land bridge". My conclusion is that European archaeologists, wishfully, liked to believe that only their European ancestors were smart enough to sail the Oceans.

The life I was leading was dangerous, there is no doubt. One day in Tulsa I had a 'little message' on my desk asking me to do some aviation work in the Atlantic. Somehow I had a strange feeling that I just didn't want to do this particular job. It was the first time I had such a spooky feeling. However, as I went to get my bags one of my good friends walked in and said "no problem Scott, I'll take it, my bags are packed". He went on my flight, and was never seen again. I guess only the survivors get to write stories like this. It made me feel terrible.

In Tulsa I had acquired a number of friends in the Unitarian Church and I often visited with them. One time they invited me to a young adults meeting in Dallas, Texas. This turned out to be the beginning of the most dangerous and strange experience of my life.

11

MARRIED UNDER QUESTIONABLE CIRCUMSTANCES

EAR READERS SIMPLY skip over this chapter if you wish. For me it is not pleasant to write, but it is essential to knowing more about me and why I did certain things. For example: why I spent so much time in the wilderness with friends. In addition I have decided to write this chapter as a single complete chapter rather than attempting to integrate it into the main text of the book. It is the story of unknowingly marrying a woman who was a paranoid-schizophrenic.

One by one my friends doing "soldier of fortune" work seemed to die. Airplane crashes were prominent. One good friend went down in the ocean in a helicopter and died from the cold before a rescue could be made. I myself almost succumbed to the bite of some poisonous tropical thing that bit me one night in my sleeping bag. At least I was so delirious that I was ready to jump out of a moving army truck and die at the side of the road. Later on the delirium continued and I thought that there was a beautiful nurse at my side taking care of me. In reality there were no beautiful nurses, but it must have been some kind of a sick warning of things to come.

Once, while in the United States, I was invited to a Unitarian Church conference in Dallas, Texas. There were lots of people there close to my age who were involved in the Church. Very shortly a woman from Tulsa, Oklahoma attached herself to me and ran off all my old friends. Her name was Merrill a person from the Shell Oil Company in Tulsa.

When I returned to Tulsa I immediately had a call from Merrill. It was an invitation to her apartment for dinner. I can't remember much about the dinner, but I can remember her inviting me to her Murphy bed immediately after. Being a red blooded man I never refused such an open invitation!

And invitation followed invitation. Soon she invited both her parents, and mine, to a wedding ceremony in Tulsa. Very honestly I had never asked her to marry me as she seemed, just different, in a strange way. Regardless, all the plans were made and the date was set while I was gone. I found out all the details later when Merrill told me she had 'just been helping me out'. The parents arrived, and that night she said "you haven't asked me to marry you, I want to hear the words!"

At this point I made a far reaching rationalization in my mind saying "Every one around me is dying, I may not last much longer. What the hell, why not get married!"

At the time I had a sure and positive belief that I would never live past 30 years of age. The feeling was so strong that nothing could seem to shake it off. Perhaps this just goes along with doing dangerous jobs. The result was that I got married in the Unitarian ministers house in Tulsa.

The previous night I had driven past Merrill's office building downtown. It normally had a large illuminated sign running vertically on the front of the building that said "SHELL". That night the lights in the "S" letter had all burned out and the sign said only a very emphatic "HELL". It was to be a chilling forecast of my life to come with Merrill. I simply didn't know it.

My life nonetheless was mostly away from Tulsa. At one point I did invite Merrill to a field project that happened to be in the United States. We spent just a few days together at Cameron, Louisana. We did manage to make a baby on the floor of an army tent at my project. Shortly after that the tent and everything in it burned to the ground. This was perhaps another bizarre prophecy.

After my project was finished I retired from my job in Tulsa, and from my military overseas work, in favor of returning to college full time. During the summer, just before school started, we had a child we named RobTom Harden. The Tom was for one of my favorite uncles. I soon discovered our baby had picked up some infection at the hospital causing quarter size pus sacks all over his body. Merrill solved the problem by simply rejecting the poor baby as though he did not exist at all. Therefore it was up to me to take care of the unlucky baby, to remove the pus sacks, clean, and dress the wounds all alone. Rob-Tom survived his first major illness.

Shortly after we had another baby named Dianna. She was the light of her mother's eye and could do no wrong. Indeed her mother insisted in feeding her with baby bottles having nipples with knitting needle sized holes instead of traditional "mother's milk". The poor child was drownding in milk, but Merrill continually insisted that I was secretly starving my poor daughter when I replaced the nipples with those having normal sized perforations. She would secretly replace them again, and again, with the monster hole nipples, as soon as I was out of sight, to foil my alleged plot against my daughter. Thus is the thinking of a true paranoid schizophrenic.

As a result Dianna learned to keep her tongue at the front of her mouth to keeping from drowning in milk. Later on she had awful speech defects due to her mother's drowning her in bottled milk.

Rob-Tom meanwhile was continually manipulated and tricked by his mother. He had tantrums of screaming and hitting. I found that, remarkably, they only started about a half hour before I was expected home. Merrill had developed clever techniques for goading the poor child into the tantrums to show me how bad he really was. There seemed to be nothing I could do to stop this horrible child abuse. My skills in psychiatry were totally lacking.

Talking to Merrill about any kind of problem was totally useless. She simply became "deaf" and would look blankly at me. I knew she could hear me, but it did no good as she was psychologically deaf. I think she knew from childhood experience that literally "turning deaf ear" to anything she did not want to talk about was one extremely effective way to avoid denouement, at least from her point of view. Rational people do not know what to do when another person simply acts deaf and looks blank in response to each question. A rational person simply gives up trying to question a deaf person.

I went to my father, a medical doctor, for help. He had never studied psychology for some reason, otherwise his answers might have been different. His answer was "wait a while and the problems with Merrill will go away". This was not a real solution, and the problems only got worse, much worse.

For Merrill the world was not logical and she knew that she was different than other people. She knew this and had an alternate solution. She would memorize passages from books that other people told her were "normal" books. I discovered this when I noticed her answers to me often sounded like they came directly from a book. One day I confronted her with this idea and astoundingly her answer was "yes, that is from page 93 of XXX book on the upper part of the page". I checked this reference and found she had truly memorized the passage perfectly. I still remember the page number!

Merrill's world was strange and frustrating to her. Nothing in her world was logical. Therefore when things did not come out the way she expected it was entirely the fault of the nearest person. People were always trying to do things to her. I understand that she once interpreted Johnnie's hamburger wrappers on her lawn as a secret plot against her by Johnnie's and she tore up the burger stand, thus ending up in jail.

I began to have trouble with my employers due to Merrill's paranoia. Again and again Merrill would get me fired by telling my boss very confidentially, by a whisper in his ear, that I was secretly doing bad things against him. She was quite convincing too. Merrill never reasoned out the fact that if I lost my job it would hurt her too.

Three times at a parties she took my bosses aside when they were slightly drunk and told them very confidentially, I was doing something very bad, secretly against both him, and the company. Each time it took a long time to find out what had actually happened. Usually I would loose my job before the fact of insanity came out. Usually the boss was so up tight over the reasons Merrill fantasized, that he would not tell me why I was being fired. This is quite reasonable since the rationales Merrill gave were really the thoughts of a totally insane person. But in those days neither I, nor my bosses, suspected insanity was the true nature of the trouble.

Meanwhile strange things started happening to me at the dinner table. For some reason I would get sharp pieces of glass in my food. Later on after reading Merrill a magazine article about people getting steel splinters in their food, in the old days, I started getting steel splinters in my food too. Long sharp splinters. Merrill, on hard questioning, had recently decided fantastically she was not smart enough to use modern can openers, and she had reverted to a very old fashioned type of can opener that always produced steel splinters. This did not explain to me why the deadly items only appeared in my food, and never hers, or the children's. This was where my eyes began to open as to the fact she was a deadly threat.

Over and over Merrill would believe that I was trying to do things to kill her. One strange event happened after I put a lightning rod system on the mountain top house to protect my radio amateur equipment. She insanely rationalized that it was really designed to attract lightning to kill her. When the first storm appeared she immediately left the house and wandered around outdoors in the rain waiting for the lightning to hit the house. Rather lightning hit a tree near her and started a fire at the base. She immediately came indoors and steadfastly refused to further talk about why she was out in the electrical storm.

I never knew what was truth and what was fantasy with Merrill. I liked cats and dogs and had a number. Often I would come home and find one of my cats in the bath tub bleeding. Another time I found cat scat all over the kitchen walls from it being kicked violently. Yet another cat was simply run over. Apparently in a moment of psychotic frustration she would violently kick any animal in her path. Frustrations came often to Merrill, but always, always, in secret.

Schizophrenic thinking was mirrored in Merrill's actions at a picnic one day. Paper cups were blowing in the wind so she stabbed a knife through each into the table top. Then she was astounded that they would not hold soda pop! Schizophrenics just can't make logical conclusions, and this is the basis of their problem, and no doubt the cause of their paranoia, but I have said this before.

In addition to other problems Merrill would write letters that were strange. She would regularly attribute these weird writings to other people, or simply could not hear questions about the letters. Rational people of course would be stopped cold by her responses, something I can understand.

Later when I was living in Washington, D.C. Merrill came to the city and went up and down the street obtaining neighbor's addresses. She then sent each neighbor letters so weirdly sexually explicit that no one wanted to talk about the mail. At last I did see a copy of her mail and found it to be aberrant beyond any rational persons comprehension. Moreover the letters had a doctors name and return address, yet they were all clearly in Merrill's own handwriting.

I believed she was dangerous, seriously dangerous. Once when I was fishing in a very open area beside the road in Alaska someone hid in the bushes about 200 yards away and took twenty shots at me. The first bullet passed close enough to my ear that it was deafening. I yelled for the shooter to "look out where you are shooting". The next shot was also deafeningly close. At that point I dove behind a boulder that was sticking out of the mud flats. More shots rang out, but all missed, I think because the shooter was running away. Later on Merrill wrote me a letter detailing of all of the facts of the shooting attempt, but she reversed all the facts so that I was doing the shooting and she was the victim. Who else but the shooter could have known such facts?

I believe she is a dangerous woman to everyone for the good reasons I have just given. I divorced her for such reasons. Frankly I never want to have anything to do with her again. In spite of my wishes she often followed me, promising that she will never forget.

Thankfully the last problems were in Washington, D.C. where she repeatedly called my work places from Denver, Colorado. Apparently she made hundreds of psychotic calls at government expense. She would swear violently at who ever answered the telephone and scream obscenities about me. My company asked me to stop her, but I was powerless being no longer being married to her. I took the problem to a Washington lawyer and he found that although you can write anything in a letter you not do that on the phone. Moreover the phones she used were federal government phones. The FBI was brought into the case and the phone calls stopped.

What happens next is unknown, but shoes are always waiting to drop.

12

SCHOOL AGAIN

WITH THE TRANSITION to married life I decided that I had better return to college and finish my degree. When on a trip to Illinois to visit my parents I discovered Rockford University at Rockford, Illinois. Friends gave this college very high ratings and said the staff was first rate. Later they were proved right, the college was everything they said and more. The really special thing about Rockford University was that it previously was an exclusive woman's college that had just decided to admit men. The most notable alumnus was the well known social worker Jane Adams.

What more can I say here... there were no toilets for men! That little problem changed fast, even though it was not exactly on the top of the college priority list. I know women will get a laugh out of male equality being turned inside out this way, but that is the way it truly was!

Candidly women at the college were remarkably aggressive. The women worked very competitively against each other to get good grades. Actually I was tremendously pleased to see how the women were actually behaving in a women's college. I am pretty dumb about women, but I was astounded and disappointed that within two years much of the competitiveness seemed to disappear in favor of women being more subservient to men.

College started and I did quite well particularly in physics and chemistry. It was time to take a lot of math since I was a bit behind most of the other physics majors in this subject. My teachers were superior in every subject. My class mates were always helpful in every way, and my grades did well. It was a very happy circumstance to have selected such a good college.

It was fascinating to actually analyze chemicals in the lab. This had been a childhood interest and I did extremely well. Perhaps even my fathers dinning table discussions had something to do with it too, I don't know. In any case I really enjoyed chemistry.

One of the memories of chemistry lab was the day that a student built a large pile of zinc and sulfur then touched it off with a Bunsen burner. Suddenly there was a bright flame from his side of the room. This was followed with dense clouds of white smoke, so thick we couldn't see to get out of the room. It was mostly by feel that all of us made our way to the door. That was the end of class that day!

But physics was my major and atomic physics was very important since it was only about thirteen years since the first atomic bombs were exploded. There were endless exciting classes and lab projects with various types of radioactive chemicals. Geiger counters were something I really understood since they were electronic. My teachers were truly good and they made the subjects especially exciting.

To complete my degree I was forced to take some subjects that I had never thought much about. One such subject was Optics. Again, like everything in physics, it was largely mathematical. Because of the math connection I could easily understand what was happening in Optics. I still remember experiments with twisting of polarized light shown through various organic liquids. My teacher was Dr. Mildred Bulliet and she made the subject particularly fascinating.

Occasionally Dr. Bulliet would invite me to her house for parties. Her husband was also an extraordinarily interesting person too since he had been an engineer designing and drilling the bores of large military canons, he had also been a U.S. to Moscow technical contact for the Communist Russians during World War II, and he had in addition had been literary critic for the New York Times newspaper. I had never met a person of such broad interests before.

No wonder I refused a very good offer from the chief engineer of the Quick Clutch Company in Rockford to go to work for them full time. Years later I would meet the same engineer in Anchorage, Alaska.

However, I worked part time at the Rockford Airport as an inventor's assistant. A man there had inherited a large sum of money which he used to set himself up as a professional inventor. I think he had lots of fun doing it in his 20,000 square foot private laboratory near the airplane hangars. He would come into his lab just after lunch and work on until late at night. Often he would spend the night on the leather couch in his private library.

I helped out with the electronic things. Since it was at the very beginning days of microwave ovens and frozen foods my task was to design and build a special super power microwave oven which would flash cook an entire dinner in five seconds. At least that was the plan. Honestly no one really knew what would happen, or if it could be done.

As I remember I designed a 5,000 Watt transmitter operating on 800 megahertz, and it worked great. Well we sure did learn a lot about how long it would take to correctly cook each part of a frozen dinner. There were exploding peas, steaming mashed potatoes that were still frozen on the inside, meat that had frozen sections adjacent to red hot pieces of gristle. Wow, did we learn a lot about cooking! It was physics in a way. Frankly the oven was not a success, we simply had more expectations than were realistic. At least no one else to this day has ever been able to cook a dinner in five seconds, so I guess I have no regrets.

The Communist Russians had just put up a small satellite and the whole world was astounded. You could even go out at night and see the flash of the Communist Russian rocket body in the sunlight when it passed overhead. We radio amateurs could listen to the Communist Russian radio signals with ease. Those facts made space travel real to even the least scientific persons. It was a time when the whole scientific and educational world was turned upside down.

Almost immediately all college science courses became very extremely serious. Math also became a critical adjunct subject to all science students. Rockets and satellites were somehow the most interesting themes of every respectable science professor. One particular professor at the State University of Iowa named Dr. Robert van Wagnen was way ahead of them all. He had already designed and helped launch the first United States satellite. He was without doubt the national hero of the moment and particularly the hero of every physics student.

13

THE FIRST SATELLITES

WITH TWO MORE years of successful college and good grades under my belt at Rockford Univercity I used my summer vacation to go to the State University of Iowa (S.U.I.) and interview with Dr. Van Wagnen. I was able to wangle a job as physics lab assistant to Dr. Van Wagnen for my fifth college year. In addition I became a full time S.U.I. physics student.

We moved our house trailer to Iowa City, Iowa and set up housekeeping in one of the trailer parks near the wide river that passed through the city. Every day I would go off to work and to my classes at the State University of Iowa. But all was not without problems.

The University required that everyone take a special S.U.I. entrance intelligence test to enter the college. This test apparently was a money maker for the University, and besides it was the cherished baby developed by one of their staff. Remarkably the test questions were all based on the time period at the end of World War II, a period I remembered well. Moreover I took the test as an adult four year college student in a large room full of freshmen students' fresh out of high school. At any rate the University promptly lost my test scores.

So back for another test, and of course I had to pay again. Remarkably it turned out to be exactly the same test questions as the first one I had already taken. The results were the same too. The University lost my test scores, again!

Back for a third test! Remember, I was a lot older than anyone else taking this particular test, and that I had already had four years of college. Moreover I had pretty well memorized the test the first two times I had taken it. The University randomly selected another test for me to take. Chance was strangely on my side as it turned out to be exactly the same test I had already taken twice before. Naturally I zipped right through the test in no time at all. Not remarkably unusual, I also got 100% on the test. According to the test's designer it was "absolutely impossible for anyone to get 100% on my intelligence test!". With a red face he threw me out of the testing facility promising to end my college career for cheating.

Perhaps my letter to The University debating the value of giving this test to older adults who had already taken it twice before helped my case. At any rate The University forgot all about the alleged cheating and everything proceeded well from that point on. I became an official student.

Being in the physics department at S.U.I. at this particular time was fascinating and exciting. The world was looking to S.U.I. as a leader in physics. Many classes were jammed with foreign students, but the Chinese were perhaps the most interesting. Like me they were older than the normal Iowa college student, but their method of learning was quite different by my American standards. They memorized everything word for word rather than using a logical approach. Their papers and tests were pure memorization efforts. Chinese did not like laboratory classes, as they did not do well working with actual equipment. I learned that obviously things were different in China than they were in Iowa.

My classes were mostly physics again. A couple of them were different, one class I enrolled in was in graduate level geology, and another in second year German. Since I had only one other class in geology I asked the professor if he thought that I should really take such an advanced class in United States Geology. His answer was "sure". Perhaps he just needed a few extra students to fill up his quota, I don't know. It was a bit of a shock to find that I was one of only two of his students who were not graduate geologists. My compatriot non geologist was a medical student who also had a private interest in geology.

I still remember being assigned a term paper on 'The Geology of The State of Alabama'. This was probably the only state I had not visited and had no real clue about their geology. Working on this paper required a lot of heavy library research, and a lot of writing. It was pure sweat as far as I was concerned. I worried over the paper tremendously as I was competing with a room full of professional graduate geologists. Luckily my professor took pity on me and passed me none the less.

One of the things about obtaining a physics degree at this time was that it was necessary to read, write, and speak a modest amount of German to become a physicist. The very minimum requirement was two years of German classes. Merrill had come from a German speaking family. Sometimes we would speak German in our trailer home too. Since I had already had one year at Rockford I mistakenly thought that another year would be almost a cinch. It wasn't!

Joining with my German classmates on the first day I was astounded to find them speaking to each other in excellent German before the professor made his entry. Conspicuously their spoken German was not just ordinary German, but a philosophical German, that most difficult special branch of the German language where you can say things you can't even think in English! It turned out that Iowa City, Iowa was an area where there were a large number of German religious immigrants, who still spoke German at home, in church, and in their daily religious philosophical discussions. Needless to say my German class was another laborious class.

The place at S.U.I. where I had real fun was in the basement of the physics building. Dr. Van Wagnen gave me a desk and a large office which I shared with four other physics students. Today one is the head of the S.U.I. physics department, and another I understand is the head of a large Swedish university physics department. The third was the captain of the foot ball team and running a fascinating experiment on pulsations in the earth's magnetic field. In any case in those days three of us were also working on the explorer series of satellites. The National Aeronautics and Space Administration (NASA) had just barely been organized by the United States., and the U.S. Army had their own intercontinental ballistic missile organization in Alabama. However, we S.U.I. students were the real non Russian experts on satellites.

Dr. Van Wagnen had a long standing interest in high altitude atmospheric physics. He previously had built a number of electronic rocket pay loads used to study the northern lights and radiation in the earth's ionosphere. These early rocket pay loads were made from things like radio tubes, mechanical relays, resistors and capacitors, and launched into the upper atmosphere on large surplus military anti- aircraft rockets.

In order to get scientific information on the aurora the rockets were launched from Churchill on Hudson's Bay in Northern Canada. They actually went clear out of the earth's atmosphere and into space before returning to earth. The Hudson's Bay site is near the north magnetic pole and it has good auroral activity all year long. This early space research prepared Van Wagnen for the International Geophysical Year (I.G.Y.), and prepared him to be the only real potential satellite expert in the United States at the time.

The United States supported the I.G.Y. as a scientific project, but it was not a particularly important project in the public, or governmental eyes. The U.S. was to launch a low cost, multi-stage, rocket designed by various marginally funded universities. The Communist Russians on the other hand had launched using large military rockets, and had fully funded military project and engineers. The pay load at the top of the American rocket was to be a grape fruit shaped satellite which would orbit the earth studying radiation around the earth. This satellite was to be built by Dr. Van Wagnen and his students, it was derived from his earlier experiments in Canada.

After the Communist Russians launched their satellite, and the U.S. had nothing but disastrous launch failures with their early satellites, there was evident governmental panic. People were saying 'perhaps the U.S. was not the world leader in science after all'. Still with great effort, and a certain amount of luck, the U.S. finally was able to put one of Van Wagnen's grape fruit sized satellites into orbit. As I have said, it was based on the Hudson's Bay rocket pay load designs, slightly updated. However, the Communist Russians had already stolen the leed, and the real scientific thunder.

Parts of the I.G.Y. space program were shifted over to the Army. Werner Von Braun, German World War II V2 rocket expert, was nominally in charge of the Army's rocket program at that time.

With world satellite competition now being of great importance, and NASA not yet functioning, Van Wagnen was asked to design a new satellite series which would be launched on top of the Army's Redstone rocket. This was to be the Explorer series of satellites.

When I was in the physics department Dr. Van Wagnen obtained a second contract to build four satellites. The price was only $40,000. Dollars. This meant that each satellite was worth $10,000. Dollars. By today's standards this is an astoundingly economical price when compared with present multi-millions of dollars now spent on a single modest satellite!!! Well, student labor at $2. Dollars an hour was cheaper than NASA labor, and there was no padding of the prices by the University either.

Laboratory assistants, like me, designed and built an entire satellite with a Geiger counter, particle detectors, a complete telemetry system, a 70 milliwatt radio transmitter, and more, for launch into space. The Explorer series of satellites were about 8 inch diameter cylinders and about four feet long. They were attached to a similar diameter solid fuel rocket, also about four feet long. Four rod antennas projected from the center of the combined package.

I built up the Geiger counter and pulse count divider systems on circular epoxy-glass boards the same diameter as the rocket. Each component I used was tested then mounted and soldered onto the board. This was in the days before "printed circuits" were common and much of the work was done by drilling a hole in the fiberglass board, mounting a pencil lead sized metal solder post, then I would attach the electronic parts and wires. There was a lot of hand work involved; indeed to be truthful it was all hand work. Somewhere on each satellite I would try to put my initials, or name, so I could say my name was truly in space. Indeed, in retrospect, my name will be in space for thousands of years this way, or at least until the dead bodies of the satellites fall back to earth.

Testing of each completed satellite circuit board was done by me in an oven and then on a shake table to insure that it would work properly after launch. I also tested high voltage Geiger counter power supplies in a vacuum chamber which simulated space. It was great fun watching the altitude in the chamber go up to the equivalent of being in space, or more than 100,000 feet and higher. At that kind of altitude the 1000 volt Geiger counter power supplies would start to corona, or the electricity would leak over the surface of the circuit boards, completely unlike the way things happened here on earth. Consequently I had to develop methods for controlling this type of high voltage leakage out in space. It was a valuable lesson that helped me out years later when designing extremely high voltage low frequency antennas.

The shake table tests were entertaining too. We would set up the operating satellite on an electronically driven vibrating table. We would then change vibration frequency up and down to find any weakness in the craft. The satellite electronics would almost become fuzzy to the eye as they vibrated. Afterward any broken components would be repaired.

I found that if I used loud popular music, instead of a regular swept tone, to shake the satellites I could find all the potential problems in a tenth the time of normal shake tests. However, this was my own secret private test to insure that everything was going to pass during the official test. I only ran this secret test when no official was looking, or should I say listening.

I worked on satellites for almost a year in the physics department. Sometime during this year NASA was turning into an ordinary government agency and they began to write down all of the rules for building a NASA satellite in great detail, even though they had never built one themselves. One rule was that all component attachment wires should be soldered into the satellite using exactly a 180 degree bend on the terminals. This was so that the satellite could be repaired easily with a soldering iron. I had some rather amusing arguments with NASA over the validity of satellite repair, since no human had ever been into space in those days, and of course no satellite in space had ever yet been repaired.

Before NASA had fully developed into a standard inflexible governmental establishment I would send my satellites down to Huntsville, Alabama with some of the instructions written in the German I was studying. It was a popular myth in those days that the numerous Germans, under Von Braun, were actually running the U.S. space program. Perhaps these German instructions are why Dr. Von Braun invited me to his office one day when I was in Huntsville, Alabama, I don't know. I was at his office door with his secretary when some pressing problem came up, and I never got to meet the famous rocket scientist.

During this period one of my satellites was mounted on top of the five stage Redstone rocket for launch. The bottom most stage was a liquid fuel rocket topped by four more stages of solid fuel rockets. Well, on take-off the liquid fuel rocket did not develop full power for some reason and lift off was only about fifty feet in the air. After a moment of hesitation the whole rocket fell over bursting the tanks of liquid fuel and liquid oxygen. This naturally produced one hell of a fire, and my satellite was right in the middle of it all! Someone with a wry sense of humour was kind enough to send me back the charred satellite remains in a toy rocket box. Remarkably some of the circuit boards still worked in spite of the fire.

Other strange things happened in those early days of space. One day a very large truck pulled up to front door of the physics building. They started unloading top quality oscilloscopes, dozens of them. Apparently they were donated by the Tectonics Company in recognition of the University's successful space work. Up to that time having your own oscilloscope was the dream of each graduate student. Now everyone who was anyone in the physics department could have his pick of any of the most expensive, and finest, oscilloscopes made at that time.

Space was not the only place where incredible things were happening in those days. One day a large passenger airplane took off from New York City on it's way to Washington, D.C. and blew up en route. Astoundingly I discovered that I had some sort of a bizarre connection to this disaster.

14

BACK TO THE SOUTH AMERICAN

A FOUR ENGINE COMMERCIAL airliner crashed along the Delaware coast of the United States on the way from New York City to Washington, D.C. Everyone aboard was killed. An investigation discovered that one person was missing, and that there was a hole in the fuselage where the toilet had been. It was clear that a passenger locked himself in the toilet and blew him self out through the side of the plane causing the plane to crash.

More investigation discovered that the missing passenger was a New York lawyer with a highly suspicious clientèle. Apparently he had been the money carrier for the Las Vegas mob among other things. It was said that he also was light fingered with the mob's money. In addition they found he had swindled a number of hospitals and resort hotels out of large amounts of money. Basically this man was on a lot of hit lists and apparently he decided to beat the mob to the punch. He had taken out an exceptionally large insurance policy in the New York airport in his wife's name. He then boarded the plane.

Now this lawyer just happened to be married to a top magazine cover girl and well known New York model by the name of Jan Klein. Yes, the same woman I had dated and worked with on the steam ship South American. Even though I had not seen her for eight years a lot of people still remembered how close we were on the ship. A lot of those people also wanted to know how I fit into the airliner catastrophe.

I had to tell everyone that I had absolutely no connection what so ever to Jan Klein since I left the ship. Among the people wanting to know all the possible spicy detail were the steam ship line people I had sailed with as radio officer in 1952. They believed me, and they were quite friendly. In fact they offered me a job as radio officer for the 1960 sailing season on the Great Lakes.

By the spring of 1960 academic studies had just about burned me out. Satellite construction was nearly finished for the Explorer series of space craft that I had been building. Merrill was acting very strangely too. Consequently I wanted to get away, and this was the perfect chance. I could sail the Great Lakes for the summer season, send the money home, and decide what would be done for work in the fall of the year.

I was assigned to the S.S. South American leaving from Detroit, Michigan. I flew over to meet my ship and become Second Radio Officer. It was good to have the two gold stripes on my sleeve. The Third Radio Officer was Tony Officer, a tall Greek with a strong religious nature. The First Radio Officer was Frank Arnold, an older fellow who had been a World News photographer for many years, and on occasion a radio officer on various ships.

The "South" sailed full of passengers. Our cruises on the Lakes were always enjoyable. Also Frank was full of stories about meeting various movie stars and other notables during his days as a news photographer. Just to prove it he had a file of "special" photographs of many of the stars. Some were R rated. Things like starlets with the wind blowing their skirts high enough to let Frank's camera discover that they had no panties. Naturally I always looked forward to a 'show and tell' session by Frank.

The college age crew of the ship would go ashore to a favourite bar in each port. I always tried to limit my drinking, but I did enjoy the trips ashore and we did have good times. Tony on the other hand would go ashore at each port and visit a church. Frank and I decided to tell him big stories about our wild and drunken times ashore, and Tony would believe them all. At each port Tony would spend his time ashore praying for us sinners, at least that is what he told us.

My time on the S.S. South American was tremendously relaxing after all the university studies and the intense full time work in the physics lab. Our route was from Buffalo, New York, to Cleveland,

Ohio, to Detroit, Michigan, to Mackinac Island up where all the Great Lakes come together, then through the Canadian "Soo" Locks, to Houghton, Michigan, and lastly to the farthest end of Lake Superior, to Duluth, Minnesota. Trips were timed to allow the passengers to visit each port during the daytimes, and for them to have enough time to wander through the shore side shops.

The old time professional sailors simply wandered up and down the streets of the towns looking in store windows. They seldom spent much time in bars, or in buying souvenirs to send home. They had been to every port anyway, and their families needed the money they might spend home. I'll admit we college students did tend toward visiting occasional bars and buying some little things.

As I remember I would stop in at all of the antique book shops in Buffalo. I found Cleveland a worthless place to visit, early Sunday mornings even though my Friend Emma lived there, and we never even talked on the phone. The Detroit water front always called for a trip to the Tastie's ginger ale factory store for a sip of the world's best ginger ale. In those days it was aged in wood and had a taste unlike any other. Mackinac Island was the place where I would wander up and down the street and watch the passengers take rides in horse drawn carriages. Before going back to the ship I also would stop at Mona's fudge shop and get something for my sweet tooth. In the "Soo" I might sneak ashore and get a few groceries for the Radio Officers. Houghton was a place to explore, they had beautiful hollyhocks, an interesting local brewery, and the university had the largest copper nugget in their lawn that I had ever seen.

Our shipping company operated out of Detroit since we passed through there twice a week. Here is where the ship would take on groceries to feed the passengers. Often I had "port watch" and had to stay on board the ship. There were always strange events for my eyes at Detroit. Every trip I noticed that a well dressed gentleman would push fully loaded hand carts full of vegetables on board the ship. One of the men on the bridge told me that he was actually a millionaire and owned one of the local banks, and also the food supply company. He said that the man just enjoyed being with the working men and doing some physical labour.

Another time Detroit showed it's truly dark side. There were many shootings and murders in the city in those days. One shop I visited down by the docks showed me bullet holes in one of their interior doors. But one day as I stood my "port watch" I looked down in the water flowing past the ship. What should I see there but a head floating down the river with it's dead eye sockets looking up at me with a ugly ghostly stare. By the time I ran to get a gaff to snare the head it had floated well out of my reach in the rapid current of the Detroit River.

Perhaps Detroit was cursed for me. Toward the end of the summer season I received a hand written personal letter from Merrill when we docked at Detroit telling me that she was leaving me. I explained the problem to the officers on the ship and immediately went to the Detroit airport.

The flight to Chicago was short and I took a taxi to where Merrill was staying. She looked surprised to see me. I asked about the letter, and with a totally blank face she said "what letter, I didn't send you a letter". This was probably my first realization of the depth of her insanity. However, I will admit my own tendency was to reject this sort of problem when I probably should not have done so.

15

OFF TO SOUTH AMERICA

Here I was in Chicago with an insane wife, and two children, and no job. Astoundingly Merrill had no memory of writing the "dear John letter". However, I was to find out that her memory was indeed excellent, but she would assume other personalities in order to do things that only could be considered insane. Then she could say, with some kind of perverted truth, "I didn't do it, someone else did it!". So in spite of Merrill I needed a job quick.

I called my old employers at Hyperac Service Corporation down in Tulsa, Oklahoma. They said yes they would be very glad to get me back, come on down. I put all our things in a "U-Haul" van and drove back to Tulsa after three years away.

Once there I looked for a house and found one on South Sandusky Street only one block off famous Route 66. The cost in those days was pretty stiff for an ex-student at twelve thousand dollars, but that was 1961. Incidentally I drove past the same house in 1997 and it looked identical to the way I had bought it some thirty six years earlier.

This was an "interesting" house since it was infested with hordes of cockroaches. The first night I was there I walked into the kitchen and switched on the lights. It seemed the whole place was covered with millions of cockroaches. They all ran for the cover of cupboards, walls, and any crevice available. A few days later I decided to use poison gas on them. I bought a pound of powdered sulphur. This was piled on the ends of four beer cans placed in iron pans, all distributed evenly on the kitchen floor. The sulphur was ignited and I took the family out for a twenty four hour trip into the country while the sulphur dioxide did it's work. When we came back all the cockroaches were dead and gone for good.

After this experience I tore out the kitchen cabinets and walls. Inside cavities were several bushels of cockroach egg cases. I presumed it was result of years of accumulation. I rebuilt everything and tightly sealed all cracks and holes. My mother sent me a very large professionally done mural for the wall and everything in the kitchen was made new and sparkling. The roaches and their unique smell were gone, I hope forever.

Most of the time I was working in the research laboratory in Tulsa. I was developing a new type of high power wide band radio transmitter system. This would send out several long range navigation signals simultaneously without retuning. Two of these transmitters would then be combined and broadcast four frequencies from a single antenna. It was a difficult job since any power leaking from one transmitter into the others would generate spurious signals and broadcast unwanted and illegal signals. It was just like putting two standard broadcast stations on adjacent channels on a single antenna. This sounds simple to the uninitiated but it is a very demanding mathematically intensive engineering task.

Somehow I had also earlier acquired the reputation of being an international trouble shooter: One of those rare people with plenty of experience who can solve any problem, anywhere in the world.

I had a sudden rush call to go to the South American country of Surname to get a party of men out of a lot of trouble. This time I flew with the old Pan American Airways from country to country. It was a long flight on the four engine piston airplanes used in those days. Tulsa to Kansas City, to New York, to Miami, to Puerto Rico, to Trinidad, to Guyana, then to Surname, as I said it was a long trip.

Right off things were bad for me. The plane landed on a old World War II airport cut into the jungle a considerable distance from any city. On arrival I didn't have a passport or visa since it was such an urgent project. The security police at the airport put me in their jail and I was feeling pretty much abandoned. About then a man walked past the locked gate of my jail cell and said in Dutch

"John Chen wants to see him". The results were electrifying and almost instantaneous. I was released immediately and given the VIP treatment by the police.

I was met by a member of the group that was in trouble and he took me on into the capital city, Paramaribo. I got a room at the largest hotel in town and I promptly got severely sick. It was a horrible sickness that produced continual vomiting and diarrhea. Perhaps it was some kind of cholera, but who knows. I was worried about electrolyte imbalance putting me permanently in the local grave yard so I drank all the water I could. Later on some of my people found a man that passed for a "doctor" and got him to come to the hotel and see what he could do for me.

This "doctor" sat on my bed since I couldn't raise my head and cracked jokes in Spanish. Actually I didn't think his jokes were the least bit funny, particularly in my condition. He also told me that he became a "doctor" by being a "nurse" for two years in Venezuela. With this "remarkable" medical background, and a rusty tin box of unsterilized hypodermic needles he decided that I needed a shot of some type of morphine to stop up my gut. Remarkably the "cure" worked, but I was extremely weak for several days after this. It was surely a great way for the new "trouble shooter" to hit town!

Trouble came in other ways too. The crew in Surname was there to set up a radio navigation system to help find oil for the head of the country. They simply could not make their system work, particularly with the heavy static from the daily equatorial electrical storms.

I traveled back through the jungles and crossed wide rivers in small boats to look at the various stations. The land was similar to the near by Amazon River area, with jungle, trees, and swamps, full of strange things. Everything was out to kill you. There were electric eels, electric catfish, and electric sting rays that could shock the life out of you. There were fish that would eat you alive, snakes of immense size, and always poisonous insects. There were even ordinary looking trees that oozed poisonous sap that had all the lethality of military mustard gas. The local saying was that if you lay down under one of those trees you would never awake. I will vouch for the fact that one invisible drop of the sap blowing in the wind will produce a blister the size of a bottle cap.

If the jungle didn't kill you then the inhabitants were of such a mind. Many Africans brought to the country a century earlier had escaped slavery by disappearing into the jungle. There they took up a life similar to Africa. Their competitors for space in the jungle were the Indigenous Indians and there were always small unnamed wars going on. Generally the local Indians and especially European whites were on their hate list. I had plenty of trouble with them, even though it was not my ancestors that enslaved them.

Then there were local political problems too. One of the three stations in our network was located in British Guyana and they were in the midst of period of social unrest. At the time Janet Rosenswieg, an old Chicago communist, had married the head of the Guyana government. However, she was more than his wife, she was apparently the real power in the country, and she was converting things to her own personal vision of communism. Most remarkably she had just shot and killed a British agent who rang her house door bell as part of an investigation into her illegal control of the country. Naturally she was acquitted because the lethal bullet was somehow lost down the drain during the autopsy.

Our station on the edge of Guyana was operating without the president's personal permission and things were plenty touchy. I had to hire a full time boatmen to stand by to spirit my station operator across the river into Surname whenever necessary. Population centers in Guyana at that time were centers for riots and killing. Somehow we were lucky and I never had to call the boatman to save my man.

One of my men in Surnam crashed on a motor cycle he was ridding down a jungle trail. It took us four days to get him air lifted out of the jungle and into the hospital at Paramaribo. You should know the hospital was a square two story building with a grassy open plaza in the middle of the square. I was asked to take him out to the middle of the open area and sit him on a chair. Then two large heavy set African women appeared. One suddenly threw her arms around him from behind, and held him tight to the chair. Before he could squirm much, the other woman put her foot on his chest, and pulled my man's broken arm into alignment. There were plenty of electrifying swear words said during the process. It was a good thing the women didn't speak English but I imagine they got the words.

Dr. John Chen was the political power in the country at that time. Since I was working for him he invited me over to his home for some dinner conversation. The place was a large colonial style home from an earlier era when Surname was a Dutch colony. I remember being offered a drink from the side board full of liquors. I looked them all over and noticed a long steady line of ants crawling up the leg of the table, across the table top, and into one of the bottles of sweet liquor. Consequently I selected a bottle without any ants, and wondered 'do ants get drunk?'.

I told Dr. Chen how things were going, and that I had solved all the troubling problems in his search for possible oil. He found I was a physicist and he questioned me extensively about atomic bombs and atomic power. Somehow I think I became Surinam's first informal "National Atomic Committee" of one. My strongest suggestion was "don't get this country into the atomic business".

While in Paramaribo I had an offer from a uniformed member of the nearby Surname DeBeers Diamond Mine to come and visit their mine in the interior. He said I would have to fly in on their plane as there were no roads and all arrivals were tightly controlled by their uniformed private army. Only friends like me could get in. He also said they were getting several million carats of diamonds a year and it would be an interesting trip. Since urgent business was pressing me elsewhere I had to turn down his offer and I have always regretted it.

I asked around to see if there were any uncut diamonds available on the streets of Paramaribo. The answer was "don't even ask, it can get you killed". On the streets the rumor was that all the South American diamonds were sent off to Belgium to be "reborn" as African diamonds. This was logical I guess since African diamonds were said to sell for much more than South American diamonds.

While asking about diamonds I found out that I could buy gold nuggets, but I was warned not to tell how I got them. I purchased several and took them back to Merrill. They have never been seen of since.

On one of my trips to South America I had to fly back to the United States on some small irregular airline. They stopped in Havana, Cuba. Everyone had to get off the airplane and be searched. Two of us were found without passports, and in those days of Castro's greatest power, being a U.S. citizen was a real bad thing. They immediately threw me into jail.

I remember the jail cell was white washed concrete without water or food, but again with a hole in the floor for a toilet. The bars on the doors were quite impressive from the inside. The single window was also barred but looked out onto another bullet marked white washed wall. The guards would tell me nothing, either in Spanish or in English. For one I was getting pretty worried.

Suddenly without notice a couple of very muscular guards dragged me from the cell and took me to the Havana airport. There they literally threw me on to a twin engine C47 airplane full of trash and with no seats. Only after the airplane took off did I find it was going to New Orleans from communist Cuba where I was dragged off the plane and into a large empty room in the airport. Somehow news of my coming had trigered off some unnamed government agency and they were ready for excapees. I was sat in a hard chair in the middle of a large empty room while a cadre of perhaps ten men questioned us. Their method was to march around screaming questions at the top of their voices. They would never tell who they were.

After hours of screaming I guess they were getting tired of the same answers. One by one they left the questioning room, probably for a "potty break" I thought. After perhaps thirty minutes no one had returned, so I took the bull by the horns and just walked out. No one stopped me, and I kept on going. Luckily I still had a credit card hidden, glued to my foot, and was able to get back to Tulsa.

Shortly after this I was sent to Miami, Florida to do a different job. The trouble with this was no one was quite sure what the job was supposed to be. I was just to go and meet Max Grossman, one of my old friends. Max had a motel room in one of the many towns along the Atlantic coast of Florida. He also had set up a small short wave radio station in his motel room so he could talk to me at sea wherever I would be. In any case he said that I should go to a port city and meet the skipper of a boat called "The Powership".

Strange things were happening in Florida in those days. Thousands of refugees were pouring into Miami from Cuba. The downtown streets were thronged with people just wandering to and fro. There were no cars on the streets. No one spoke English and every store had massive stacks of Spanish to English dictionaries as their chief sale item. Also there were long lines of men in front of certain houses that were said to be recruiting stations for an army to invade Cuba.

Back at the port we provisioned the fifty foot boat "Powership" for a long trip at sea. This boat was a former military "Landing Craft Command" or LCC converted to look approxamently like a fishing yacht. Other ships at this same port were taking on provisions, and loads of rifles and machine guns, from unmarked trucks. The rumour was that such trucks were having a hard time simply getting to Florida because apparently local U.S. police were hijacking their gun cargos. At any rate we had plenty of World War II Japanese rifles and pistols aboard and the Captain told me he hated Castro for nationalizing his airline consisting of his two C-47 airplanes and would kill him if he had the slightest chance.

We went through the motions of testing a Hyperac navigation system south of Cape Kennedy. For some reason we were accompanied by two other boats which were barely sea worthy in the open ocean. During this period we went over to the Bahamas where the local police came on board and confiscated all the pistols. We still had the rifles and having plenty of experience I was elected to show people how to load, aim, and fire the Jap rifles.

I had converted our fishing outriggers into short wave antennas. This was by winding them with a spiral of wire almost invisible to the eye. With just the right length of wire they worked superbly. In the pilot house of the boat we had precision navigation equipment, also a SCA single side band short wave transmitter, and now also a very high frequency (VHF) aircraft radio. My daily short wave conversations with Max were pretty marginal since his motel transmitter worked poorly. Yet I found out that we were to move out into the middle of the Gulf Stream off the Communist Cuban coast and talk to any airplanes that just happened to call us on the air radio.

Because of the strong current at this point the sea was always full of waves coming at us from random directions. Every so often during the day one would appear off our stern and proceed to ride up over the stern right into the pilot house. It was lucky that I had put the radios up high and they somehow never got wet. If they had we would have been out of business. As it was only my pants got wet as I remember.

The wild waves were hard on my stomach. On rare occasions I would get sea sick, or perhaps it was the Communist Cuban rice, beans and garlic we were eating every day. One day I was making what I called "an offering to the fish" of my last meal when an airplane suddenly called us on the radio. I was slightly slow in answering and got chewed out by the pilot. He told me I was there to only provide them with precision location, and rescue if necessary, and to hell with my "feeding the fish". Perhaps he just didn't understand my language.

A few days after this I had word by radio to come ashore in Miami and fly back to Oklahoma. A few days later the ill fated Communist Cuban invasion started on the south side of Cuba at "La Baha de Puercos" or Bay of Pigs. It was a real fiasco, and I could only blame the poor results on the military amateurs. While in the Miami area I could see how the invasion was being set up and it was something that only an inexperienced New England college student would hope might work. Sadly it was pure military amateurism without help from any real experienced military personnel.

Life in Tulsa with Merrill was becoming difficult because of my constant travels. She always got into trouble when I left her alone. So when an old friend said that he would like me to come to work at Independence, Kansas for steady work and for more money I stupidly jumped at the chance.

16

ITTY BITTY THINGS

MY FRIEND, LUCKILY I can't remember his name anymore, he convinced me to apply to The Electro Corporation at Independence, Kansas for a job as engineer and manager. I went to Independence for an interview with the "Integrated Circuits" department of this company. I found the town of about 70,000 people to be a picture of middle America. At that time it was a farm town in the middle of flat Kansas agricultural land with a close knit culture stemming from the Wild West days shortly after the U.S. Civil War.

I spent my first night in town in an old hotel built about 1900 where there happened to be a local political meeting. The political women in the next room spent the night loudly singing at least 100 verses of "Roll me over in the clover, roll me over and do it again". I didn't get much sleep, but I decided that I rather liked the rather primitive culture of the small town, and thought that probably Merrill couldn't get into to much trouble here.

At the Electro Corporation I interviewed and they showed me about a manufacturing facility producing large quantities of small electronic circuits. This was in the early days of integrated circuits and their ideas of what was an integrated circuit was were different than today's. Their circuits were clusters of resistors, capacitors, and transistors piled up like tooth pick sized cordwood and soldered between two circuit boards. Yes they were small by the standards of the day, but nothing like you would find at present. The management was very enthusiastic about having me come and work with them. Apparently they had no one with much real electronic circuit experience; this area was a departure from their main line business of building only electronic thin film resistors and automobile electrical components. They offered me a substantial increase in salary over my research position at Hyperac Corporation in Tulsa.

So we sold our house at South Sandusky, street adjacent to Route 66, in Tulsa and moved up north over the Kansas border to the small town of Independence. We purchased a very good house just outside of town and adjacent to the local golf club, near a small lake, and with a woods and horse pasture in the rear. The house had belonged to the local radio station manager. It was a vast improvement over the Tulsa house.

Reporting to work at Electro Corporation was somewhat of a shock for me. My boss was a man with no education, but a "high tech" department manager none the less. The first day I discovered that his idea of management was right out of the early days of the industrial revolution. Everyone was graded on how fast they could assemble itty bitty things. His world was frantic all through the working day, from punch in time in the morning, to punch out time in the late afternoon. Nothing counted except how many parts a person had built in a day. And in his mind that certainly applied to engineers too.

Frankly as I learned more and more about the company I discovered that they were completely in the business of producing small parts for other companies. They supplied the automobile replacement electrical parts for Sears Roebuck, Montgomery Wards, Western Auto, and a number of other U.S. companies. They also provided electronic sub assemblies to military contractors and aircraft factories in nearby Kansas. The corporation was one of those that is entirely invisible to the public because all of their products were used in things that the public would almost never see. I also discovered that the company was ruled completely by the owner of Mid West Power and Light Company, his wife and book keeper, and that it was not a public company.

My part of the operation was to manage the "integrated circuits" department, a group of about fifty five people. These included mostly production line assemblers, some machine shop workers, several technicians, and a few production line managers. My department was completely separate from the remainder of the plant. This was to have interesting results later on.

The company president was a former top U.S. resistor salesman who had been hired for the position by the owner in Kansas City. He also was a pilot and very interested in flying so we had a common interest. I took many flights up to Kansas City, with him as pilot of the company's Cessna 310 twin engine aircraft. Acting as co-pilot I worried a bit when I saw the sweat on his forehead when we were on instruments. But we always seemed to survive the trip.

Once he rented a very nice twin engine DC3 aircraft and arranged a coast to coast sales trip with stops all across the United States. Our president also, very rationally, hired a professional DC3 pilot to fly this plane, and later on retained him to fly the company plane too. I remember our trip vividly even today. We made sales stops in Boston, then New York. Here we got lost on Kennedy Airport on a night take off and had to taxi back to the control tower and start all over again, after the tower controllers had properly identified our plane.

Then on to New Jersey where I remember having trouble finding some clients in Morristown because I did not pronounce the name with a very New Jersey nasal accent, using a hard "Maar" sound rather than a "Mor" as would be expected. Once I had been very fully corrected by the telephone operator everything went well. Later we flew across the entire United States and over the top of the Rocky Mountains without pressurization. I remember counting to see how many numbers I could say without running out of breath at 16,000 feet. All our flying seemed to be at night too, after the business conferences. Finally we went to Las Vegas and I got to see the town illuminated at night from the cockpit, a very fascinating sight. Then on to a large electronics show at San Francisco to finish our sales trip.

The sales trips were fun for me, but back in Kansas there was lots for me to work on too. My shop people were always at each other's throats. It was hard work to keep them from actual fist fights, but I was always able to cool things off. We developed new products on the basis of things learned on the sales trips and working with all the people was fascinating. I remember products like plug-in attenuators for telephone circuits, bomb timers for aircraft, message decoders for secret government projects, telephone electronics, and many more items. Mostly I remember that the other parts of the factory were having labor troubles, and that a union was trying to organize the workers much to the terror of our Kansas City owner.

About this time the firm sent me to Los Angles to take over a company they had just purchased in Santa Monica. This was a specialized enterprise that made "integrated circuits" on thin pieces of ceramic material using unique thick film techniques. The company was acquired by one of the vice presidents with only a little technical knowledge, but to him it looked real good. The salesman that cooked up the deal was a Russian with the nickname of "Texas Pete". When I got out to L.A. what I found was not good at all.

I found a production line with people who only spoke Spanish, and managers who only spoke German. I understood a bit of both. The production people were dressed up in gowns and looked appropriate to their supposed tasks. However, standing around and listening to the Spanish, I found that they were just passing "chips" from one production line station to the next, and around the end of the production line, and back again. I tried to get a look at the company books but the book keeper was adamant that she was working on them at home and that it would be absolutely impossible for me to see them at any time in the foreseeable future. Listening to the managers German I felt that they had little technical knowledge and were hired mainly for their inability to speak English. There seemed to be no real contracts either. What had been passed off as "big contracts with the great WBE company" turned out to be only an WBE interest in the proposed product, and nothing truly contractual. Frankly the company looked like a pure con game to me. "Texas Pete" had set everything up to look like a modern high tech company to the casual observer, and then he found a sucker.

My call back to Kansas told them that they had purchased a phoney operation and that they should take whatever they could find of value back to Kansas and cut their losses. I told them they should close the company down. After this I heard nothing for two weeks. Suddenly a call came through to me saying "close the company down.... and by the way we have fired you too, but we will give you a golden parachute to let you down easy." Hearing this news was bad. A schizophrenic wife, two children, and no job, in a very small town, this was a recipe for trouble.

Later on I received another phone call saying "The workers in the factory voted about eighty percent to unionize and the owner decided to close the entire Kansas plant and move the whole operation to West Texas. But they also said "you should know that at least your department voted ninety percent against the union." So my management style, keeping the workers informed, seemed to be popular with Kansas people if nothing else.

Having the money from my golden parachute, which was six months pay, I looked around for a job that appeared to be "interesting, with growth potential". I found one too, only fifty miles or so south in Nowata, Oklahoma, on the old Cherokee Indian reservation. The company was called Dinamo, and they built small electronic equipment for airplanes and radio stations. I was to be their vice president of engineering, at least that was what the front page of the local news paper says.

At Dinamo there were only a few workers but lots of projects and apparently real potential. My task was to engineer new products, and develop the paraphernalia to produce the equipment. The contract said I was to be paid in cash and stock.

Merrill, Rob-Tom, Dianna and I moved into a large old rental house at the edge of town. I was able to put my airplane in the hangar at the local airport. The town was populated chiefly by people supporting the local oil fields, mostly Indians, and people with Indian ancestry. In my memory it was a particularly flat, dull, drab town left over from the exciting early days of Oklahoma's oil boom.

Work at Dinamo was intense all of the time. I organized fabrication, developed and paid for a production facility from my own pocket with heavy sheet metal construction equipment. I built a photographic operation, designed new electronic equipment, and even developed a high volume printing operation. Wily Braun the company president also had an interest in a local radio station and so we built one with a studio and transmitter facility.

In spite of all the activity, pay was sporadic. Promised stock certificates some how never appeared. Payment for the heavy production machinery I had purchased never quite materialized. My final blow was the day that Merrill decided to help out at Dinamo. With her classic paranoid-schizophrenic secret thinking she convinced, an also paranoid Wiley Braun to go into a dark corner, and told him that I was secretly destroying him, and going to take the company away from him. Apparently she was very convincing, speaking one paranoid to another, because the next thing I knew was that I was fired as vice president. Moreover, Wily said we had no contract and he owed me absolutely nothing at all.

An interesting law suit resulted since I had a signed contract in hand. Wily held out for a jury trial after much legal maneuvering. I took a look at the jury list and found, most remarkably, that all of the jurors were Wily's relatives, something that could only happen in a small Oklahoma Indian town. The jury was thrown out and he settled "on the court house steps". I got my stock in the company which I put in a frame and kept on the wall as a reminder not to do such silly things again and to watch out for Merrill's insanity. As for the heavy equipment I hired a large truck and some very tough looking thugs and backed the truck into the factory. I said: "I am here to take back the equipment which I own and for which I have receipts". Suddenly Wily went back to his office, and astoundingly discovered that he had thousands of dollars in cash to pay me for my equipment. I went away with an empty truck and a full wallet. To this day Wily still uses the same types of equipment to produce his products.

But once again it was time to look for a new job. I would hope with some company that did not produce itty bitty things. This time I looked west toward Colorado.

17

OUTER SPACE RESEARCH

MY PRIVATE AIRPLANE took me west to Colorado in 1964. I had heard that Marvel-Georgia was looking for an engineer with satellite experience. Since I had worked for Dr. Robert van Wagnen at the State University of Iowa, and personally built the first U.S. satellites, I thought I might have a chance. To interview I flew out to Denver and rented a car at the airport. and went down to the large government financed rocket and space craft facility nearby just south of Denver, Colorado. I worried a lot about the personnel conditions here since the organization had just laid off 15,000 people and only 2,000 remained employed in the facility.

In spite of the truly bad economic circumstances in Colorado at the moment I was hired to work in the space research laboratory. I had no idea what was next. Actually the first thing was to move my family west and I did that. We drove out to Colorado and arrived on a Sunday. It those days Colorado had strict "blue laws" and no food place could be open on Sunday. We nearly starved and everyone was upset because there was no food to be purchased at grocery stores, nor were there hamburger stands, or restaurants open anywhere. It was our introduction to Colorado.

Colorado state had been in mostly static condition since the end of the 1849 gold mining era many years before, and worse since perhaps the economic depression of the 1930's. There were still many abandoned gold mining towns and old weathering mine buildings in the western mountains when we arrived. To get things started again the Governor had some ideas about luring high tech industries to the state. His neat plan was to promote the pleasures of the high mountains such as hiking, mountain climbing, skiing, camping, sight seeing, and similar pleasurable things in order to entice high tech industries to move to the state. He hoped these sugar covered cookies would also lure highly educated people, and modern technical industries, to the state. It did indeed work, but only very slowly. Marvel-Georgia was one of the first of the advanced technology firms to move out to Colorado, but for the moment at least their sudden layoffs were a major setback to the entire Colorado economy.

We soon found a house just west of Denver, Colorado, naturally for a very reasonable price. The whole south end of Denver and all the adjacent towns were in economic chaos due to the massive layoffs. In our sub division there were plenty of low priced houses available, we had only to select the one that fit our tight budget and bedroom requirements.

Out at the Waterton Marvel plant there were also plenty of empty desks available too and certainly there was no crowding due to the recent lay offs. Arriving at this time I was looked at with great suspicion by many of the company survivors, since I had been hired at the very bottom of the layoff. Luckily I joined a wonderful boss named Dr. Bob Sturm, and had any number of excellent co-workers to work with. We had an immense list of possible research projects associated with the race for space that was going on at that time.

A few of our projects had to do with things like designing an out of this world five mile diameter parabolic telescope dish, or developing a computer to find troubles in space vehicles, developing a height finding radar for landing on the moon, working with the astronauts in the Lunar Excursion Module or LEM, and many, many, highly secret military projects. Every day was exciting and interesting at Marvel.

One of my projects at the time was to develop a scheme to find enemy radar systems from a satellite. Working from my earlier experiences with Hyperac navigation system I was able to produce a radio frequency interferometer that was uniquely stable and problem free. I applied for a patent. In the final analysis the patent was delayed for years due to great secrecy concerns at that time. Suddenly one day, after I had almost forgotten the project, I received a thousand dollar check in the mail and notification that the patent was complete and issued, a truly pleasant surprise.

Another time I was called in as resident physicist to trouble shoot a space super gun project. Their plan was to build a gun that would shoot projectiles at perhaps 10,000 feet per second or more in space. This is perhaps 7,000 feet per second faster than most quality hunting rifles. The electrically powered gun would be able to shoot down enemy satellites and missiles in orbit around the earth, or perhaps as they were being launched. It was fired by energy stored in a room full of electrical capacitors, which exploded an elemental lithium charge turning it into lithium gas. The light weight gas would drive the bullets to an astounding velocity according to the muzzle mounted electronic speed gage. However, the big problem was that the bullets simply were not hitting the test targets.

After looking over this project it was plain to me what was happening. The tremendous velocity of the bullet down the barrel, plus the lithium gas leaking past the bullet, caused the bullet to simply evaporate into a cloud of gas before it left the gun's muzzle. The resulting high speed jet of gas appeared at the muzzle and was measured by the electronic system, but the real bullet no longer actually existed. Remarkably after my report, this project seemed to quietly disappear and as far as I know was never heard from again.

Another interesting project was to help develop solid state microwave transmitters for use in space. My thesis in college had been on voltage variable capacitance devices now known as parametric amplifiers. This involved a new form of solid state parametric amplifiers, something that was very new at that time, and remains rather an obscure field even today. In any case I was able to "play" with various types of transistor transmitters and found out about the troubles that could occur in their design due to parametrically induced oscillations. I published an article about the undesirable "parasitic" oscillations in these transmitters and showed methods that also allowed stable high powered transmitters to be designed at last. This article was widely read and copied, but sadly not much credit was ever given though it established an industry. Later on I went out for bids on the first solid state microwave transmitters for military satellites and was able to select a good contractor who had the knowledge to produce effective equipment.

Perhaps the most interesting project to me, in those early days of space, was assisting Dr. Sturm in designing an atomic powered space ship. This was to be able to travel from earth to the farthest planets, or even to another solar system many light years away. Even today this appears as pure science fiction, but it was to be a real space ship. The nuclear power plant was to power an ion jet drive system that would pull the pod through space for years on end. To avoid the contamination from nuclear waste products and radiation, the humans aboard would be both shielded and separated by perhaps a thousand feet or more from the atomic power plant. A long thin coaxial cable would connect the two parts of the space ship. We then developed one of the first computer systems that would send packets of information over a relatively simple coax cable in both directions in order that we could safely control the engine and report on it's operating condition. Today this is cutting edge computer science, but we were way ahead of them all. This was the kind of thing that seemed right out of science fiction, but honestly if the truth were found out we were probably all science fiction aficionados.

Meanwhile one of my projects had a lot of military interest. It was turned into a highly secret project that required that everyone working on it be confined to a steel "vault". We were locked in after we were admitted by an armed guard. The guard had to know us all by appearance rather than some plastic identification card. In the vault we only had first names or aliases, last names were forbidden. Desks were arranged so that you could not see what was going on at the adjacent desk. And if you looked right or left an armed guard would be immediately at your desk sternly questioning you about your real need to look at any other desk. As I said it was super secret. Later on this super secret project was to be my downfall for strange and curious reasons.

Life at home was unpleasant. Under Merrill's control we seemed to have disaster after disaster. She thought she should get a job teaching and consequently took a considerable amount of college training in order to be a licensed teacher in elementary school. When she graduated she immediately obtained a licence and work as a teacher. I remember that she went off to school and returned after the first day saying she hated it. She refused to return to school again for purely schizophrenic reasons that were never clear. Indeed in her insane way she would not even speak of the subject again, and all the training cost was down the drain.

Then there were all sorts of paranoid problems with pets at home. When Merrill was alone with them bad things just happened to them. She said one cat was inside the car engine and was killed when she started the car. Another cat was run over. A third, according to Merrill, was sick and defecated impossibly waist high on the kitchen walls. Frankly, I had the feeling that she kicked the cat in a violent rage, something that seemed to occur very often when she was alone with them. After such a rage Merrill would always throw them in the bathtub to keep the blood from covering the room. She always had an excuse, or a paranoid explanation, for what happened, but the explanations never really fit. She would say: "what part of the explanation don't you like". Then in a day or two the story would be changed to fix the part of the lie I didn't like.

At the Marvel plant I met a friend named George Gage, a fellow with Indian ancestry from Colorado. We both were interested in hunting and camping. This was the beginning of a wonderful friendship and an escape from Merrill. On weekends George and I would go fishing, camping, and hunting, depending on the season. George knew plenty of interesting locations in Colorado having lived there all his life. This was exactly what I needed to retain my sanity.

Our first outing was to climb a fourteen thousand foot high mountain to the west of Denver. I remember that George was able to almost trot up the trail to the top. On the other hand I had just come from the low country a few months earlier and had to huff and puff my way up the rocky trail. When we got to the top the view was spectacular, and I sat down on a rock to have my lunch. I pulled out my peanut butter and jam sandwich and a wave of altitude sickness came over me. This was my first experience with high altitude nausea.

Later on I found a unique road to the top of a fourteen thousand foot high mountain. I took my mother and a Mrs. Gross up the mountain by car. Both had just come out from Chicago which is near sea level. As we got higher and higher the two little old ladies acted like they were completely roaring drunk, as the altitude started to affect them. On the way down I showed them a spot where several cars had gone off the edge of the road, over a cliff and down some 2000 feet of cliff face. With their high altitude drunkenness it was a roaring good show to them. They didn't sober up until we got back down to about nine thousand feet.

With all of the hunting and fishing I got to know the mountains pretty well. My favourite spot was the area around the place called North Park, located in the north center of Colorado. George, Dr. Sturm, and I had hunted here for elk and deer quite successfully. After a while I started guiding groups of people into the general area. Our radio club was one organization, and they were always anxious to repeat my trips as often as possible.

One time we camped in the forest wilderness on the north side of Rocky Mountain National Park. Suddenly a jeep with several cases of beer in the front seat drove right through the middle of our tent camp, an unforgivable breach of local etiquette. The driver with a marijuana cigarette in his hand leaned out yelling "how do I get into the National Park?" I pointed down the river adjacent to the camp. Off he went in a great rush, and a while later we could hear his engine going zoom, zoom, zoom! After a very long hour of engine zoom noises I walked down the trail and found he had run his jeep off a small embankment directly into the river. His back bumper was hung up on the river embankment and his front bumper was on the rock in the river bottom. All four wheels were in the air and he was still zooming the engine with great vigour. At this point he told me "I can't understand why this damned jeep won't go, a jeep should be able to go anywhere out here!" Well it took only a minute for me to get him unstuck and he was never seen again.

A similar thing happened after I sold one of my four wheel drive vehicles to a man newly arrived from the east coast of the United States. He purchased the car and immediately roared off only to return a few days later saying: "The f—ing jeep you sold me is no damn good! I want my money back!" I asked "What happened?" He answered "I drove it down the middle of Boulder Creek and it just quit running!" Here you need to understand that Boulder Creek was filled with very large round boulders and no car yet built could drive down the middle of it without being destroyed. My answer to him was "Sorry" and "idiot".

After being at Marvel-Georgia for a number of years I was invited to a Christmas party at my secret project vault boss's house high in the mountains directly behind the plant. He had a very good rustic home with many acres of impressive mountain land covered with ponderosa pine trees. Merrill and the kids were invited too. The boss was somewhat drunk by the time we got there which added to my problems. Paranoid schizophrenic Merrill insisted that I take the kids off in the woods to chop down the Christmas tree our host had pointed out to them. In the meantime Merrill stayed at the boss's house and got him off in a dark corner. We went home with the tree after the party but I didn't know what the results would be.

The next day at work I discovered that my security clearance, on the project I had invented, had been withdrawn, and I was "persona non gratis". The guard at the vault turned me away. My vault boss said I was a high security risk but would say nothing more. I was out of work. For weeks after this I had no projects sent my way, and no explanations, and could only sit at my remote desk and wonder "what happened". With all this spare time I worried intensely about my ability to ever again do secret work, and I started looking for other employment. Merrill's insane paranoia had caused her to make up one more huge paranoid lie for my boss, she insisted I was secretly giving away secret information.

18

INSANITY RAISES IT'S UGLY HEAD, AGAIN

ABOUT SIXTY MILES north, at the university town of Boulder, Colorado, I found that the National Center for Research was looking for an electronic engineer. The project was to develop an advanced computerized radar station that would help investigate the internal workings of hail storms and other weather phenomenon. The people here seemed to be an intriguing group of PhD's doing some very remarkable weather research. I took the bait and agreed to go to work for Dr. William Redbank since my position doing secret work at Marvel-Georgia appeared to be dead.

Just before leaving Marvel-Georgia my vault boss told me that my secret status had been reinstated and they had found absolutely no security problems after careful investigation. He never would say what the problem was that caused my status malediction, except I knew it all started the day after Merrill had a secret closet talk, in a dark corner, with him at his party. There was absolutely no question in my mind that Merrill's paranoia insanity had struck again. In spite of my apparent resurrection I was not offered any new projects, nor was I reinstated to any of my old projects, and the shift to Boulder seemed the only rational thing to do. I moved the family into a rental house in the town of Boulder, but I was really looking for a place where I could build a house. In my mind this was going to be my final move and it was to be my last home.

Searching for really good mountain land required a topographic map to discover the roads back into the Rocky Mountains west of Boulder. Shortly I found an obscure mountain subdivision called Pine Brook Hills overlooking the prairie to the east and the highest parts of the continental divide to the west. Driving around this area I discovered a mountain top lot for sale that had a truly spectacular view west toward the divide and south down deep into Boulder Canyon too.

With considerable economic help from my father I bought the mountain land and started planning a house. Since I had never designed a house before I thought it would be a particularly interesting and educational engineering task. The weather and geologic conditions on the mountain top were investigated. Winds were said to be about 100 miles per hour several times during the year. The location was also weathered granite rock that would later prove to be a problem for water pipes and septic systems. In addition my friends told me that lightening hit mountain tops often during electrical storms.

The math for the design allowed me to design a house that would withstand a 100 mile per hour wind, and I added a 50 percent safety factor, just in case. Picture windows were designed to withstand the wind too. A lightening rod system was planned and the house electrical system was specially designed to prevent problems during storms. The detailed blue print plans were drawn up and submitted to the local permit office and they were accepted. The same plans were subsequently submitted to the subdivision architectural committee, and rejected. They insisted on larger picture windows overlooking the scenic views, something they considered very important from an artistic stand point. However, after a lot of argument and presentation of facts and figures about wind problems the drawings were accepted.

I was the building contractor and I engaged a local Indian man who had done this sort of work for last 15 years. Whenever I could manage it I would build portions of the house myself to save money. I installed the electrical system, put in the hard wood floors, did all the plumbing, and so on. Naturally I did all of the finish interior work. The living room Franklin stove chimney was put in by the unique process of shooting a hole exactly vertically through the ceiling and roof then following it up with the stove pipe. The house had a large vaulted ceiling living room–dining room, four bed rooms, a good kitchen, and a couple of baths. We had to dynamite a path through the weathered granite rock for the water pipe. This was exciting as several tons of granite gravel was blown high in the air and deposited on the roof. In addition a large boulder went high and came back down right through the front porch deck leaving a huge hole. Remarkably nothing else was damaged by the explosion. A shovel, some boards, plus hammer and nails, fixed the problems and the house was finished.

Merrill, Rob-Tom, Dianna and I moved into the house as soon as possible. Soon after moving in we had an electrical storm. As the lightening came closer, and closer, Merrill in her typical insane paranoia insisted she would go outside into the storm "because you planned the lightening rod system to kill me". She stayed outside in the rain until a lightening bolt hit a tree near her and started a fire in the pine needles at it's base. Suddenly she came back into the house and would not talk about the reason why she went out doors. At this point I began to get the clear idea that she was a true severe paranoid schizophrenic case. The insanity issue was completely impossible for me to mentally avoid any longer.

Each day at meals now I had to look at my food very carefully. Some kind of a dangerous surprise would likely be found in the way of a small rock, or worse a piece of broken glass in the food, and who knows what else. Then there was the day I ran across an article in the journal of the American Association for the Advancement of Science telling about how metal splinters were sometimes produced by opening tin cans and how they could be followed through the alimentary canal by electronic metal detectors. I stupidly happened to read this to Merrill, and lo about a week later she decided that she was a very old fashioned person who could no longer use her well designed modern electric can opener, but she could only use the type of old fashioned hand can opener that the article said produced dangerous steel splinters. Remarkably, I started getting sharp pointed steel splinters in my food almost every day. You should know that even more remarkably none of the children, or Merrill, ever got the splinters, glass, or rocks.

One day Rob-Tom, was going too fast on our mountain road. He rolled my jeep down the mountain side from a remote dirt area near out house. Luckily he was stopped by a grove of small pine trees and came to rest upside down. I thanked God that he didn't get hurt. The four wheel drive car had a rugged roll bar and he also had a good seat belt, but the jeep was a wreck. A neighbor helped me turn it upright, and to winch it back up on the road. Between us we pulled the car back to the house. There were no crowds, no passing cars, or no police. Yet remarkably a couple of weeks later Merrill suddenly told me that a policeman had come to the house and had given Rob-Tom a ticket for his long past accident and that he was in a lot of trouble. I felt that it was another of Merrill's cleverly conceived sick paranoid stories to get Rob-Tom into trouble, with me asking she could find utterly no proof of the existence of a ticket.

My mind flashed back to when Rob-Tom was born and came home from the hospital covered with puss filled boils. Merrill had refused to take care of him and I became his care giver. Later on, I now believe, she contrived many stories about him that were designed simply to get the poor child into trouble, but at the time, I swallowed each story hook, line and sinker. Each story was followed with the same pitiful words "I just can't control him, you have to stop him!". Things like this happened every day. Merrill seemed to have a special hate for men and a compulsion to make up special lies designed to promote hate for all the men in her life. If I had not been in a state of denial, or had some remarkably astute help from somewhere, I might have been able to reject the inherent faulty logic of these nearly magical schizophrenic insane stories.

As for my denial of the problem I allowed Merrill to surprise me day after day. Once when I was walking down our pitch black night time hall I ran into a solid iron bar placed exactly at my eye level. I was knocked to the floor nearly out cold. Other times doors would be left opened in unexpected places where I would run into them in the dark, or pins would be placed point up exactly where I would walk or sit on them. Things like this happened day after day. No wonder I was having panic attacks while living with Merrill. I never knew what would happen next.

Meanwhile back at UARC my job was going quite well. I designed a radar station and massive parabolic antenna to be placed in a compound with a group of about six other house sized trailers, near the small town of Grover, Colorado in the high prairie country near Laramie, Wyoming. This was to be one of the first fully computer controlled digital radar systems that produced three dimensional radar views of storms, and which would also track airplanes flying through the storms. This was a radar that pointed the way for almost all weather radar systems to follow. We used a pair of the then newly available PDP-8 computers, one was to digitize the radar signal returns and memorize received signals, and another to turn the data into video pictures for the ground controllers. The programming of the computers was done by a Dutch PhD. student named John Seagegent. His opinion of his own work was absolutely un-excelled. So much so that he eventually told his doctorate dissertation review board to go to hell, and he forgot about the PhD, or at least that is what he told me. However, he promised UARC exclusive rights to software programs he developed under their contract, and he did indeed produce a good product, but he also sold the same programs to many others to our great surprise. There were many other strange things happening at UARC.

The UARC building was an architectural masterpiece designed by the famous I.M. Best. It was remarkably boxy and made of concrete, an outstanding piece of architect's art, right at the very foot of Rocky Mountains, surrounded by pine forests, with herds of deer wandering about the grounds. The building became a tourist attraction and I often found tourists looking in the windows of my office.

Yet there were some serious practical problems with this picturesque and artistic building. Outside concrete stairs were spectacularly wide and lacking railings for support in icy weather. One winter day as Dr. Redbank and I were walking down the icy slick steps he slipped and fell down on the concrete stairs. I was unable to break his fall more than just slightly. The result was a blood clot that killed him quickly.

Redbank's project was in trouble and needed a proper leader. As an interim measure the projects business manager, a former naval captain, was appointed by UARC leaders to take over the operation. Later on Dr. Kurt Roe, who even later became president of the University of Wyoming, would intelligently replace the Captain. However, for the moment we were under the Captain's total command. He was rather badly addicted to alcohol in the form of pint sized straight gin refreshers. He also enjoyed drinking parties, which were mandatory if you really wanted things to go smoothly for you in "his" project. One time I was told that he was having a formal party at his house and that I should bring my wife. The party was quite a success in that he got fairly drunk and disappeared alone, to a secluded part of the house, with Merrill.

The next Monday when I arrived at UARC I found that the Captain had fired me. His reasons were not given, except that I was just not satisfactory for the position that had previously been going entirely favorably under Redbank. However I was to be given a salary for the remainder of my two year contract, but I was to leave UARC right away. Well this was the fourth time in a row that Merrill told some gigantic paranoid schizophrenic lie that got me fired. And it was always when she could get the project manager alone and drunk. So off I went once again to find some other employment to support my family.

Since UARC was to pay me my same salary for about a year as a settlement I decided to enroll as a graduate PhD student at the adjacent University of Colorado. I signed up for classes in advanced calculus, Boolean algebra, and computer programming. All were fascinating and enjoyable courses. Never the less my streak of bad luck was doing double time and The University completely lost my existence and my grades in their computer memory, and they even lost the fact I had ever enrolled, the result was that all the work I did, was done for naught. In way of explanation I must note that those were the early 1970's, days of student unrest, when university magnetic computer memory tapes and records were being demagnetized (or "hacked") for "revolutionary" reasons, and even campus buildings, power lines, and automobiles, were being blown up by the radical activists. Certainly the University of Colorado was a center for radical causes in those days.

Since moving would be difficult I found a position maintaining The University's seven TV studios and their TV station up on the mountain side behind UARC. I was given an office under the stands at the foot ball stadium, and another office in a building about a mile away. This was not a difficult job and I was able to audit many post doctorate courses in biological chemistry, one of their local specialties. Years previously I had produced remarkable grades in chemistry, and this was just bigger and better chemistry. In addition I was asked to teach university television classes to students.

My department at the University of Colorado never had parties and none of the university people were heavy drinkers. Thus things went along quite well, and Merrill never had a chance to use her paranoid-schizophrenic "logic" on anyone here.

About the most exciting thing that happened was the time when the rear of the adjacent administration building was blown up a few minutes before I arrived. Then there was the station wagon with six revolutionary people and a bomb in the back seat that blew up at my favorite hamburger stand. Actually there were a large number of terrorist bombs going off in the area in those days. It kept on until all the press people agreed to stop publicizing terrorists, and actually carried through on their promise. But never the less I refused to eat any more hamburgers until all of the body parts had been completely removed from the hamburger stand.

Approximately at this time an old friend from the University of Wyoming at Laramie came to me and said he would like me to apply for a position in their physics department working on an infra red telescope. I put together, a resume, or a "Curriculum Vitae" in university language, and applied for the position. It was well received and I turned in my resignation at the U. of Colorado. I planned on commuting back and forth from Boulder, Colorado to Laramie, Wyoming on a weekly basis. Merrill's paranoia could stay in Boulder.

At Laramie, I rented a house trailer from one of my employees as a secondary home. The work on the electronics of the telescope was highly interesting. The personnel at the university were also equally fascinating. One PhD was working on detecting near by magnetic monopoles or magnetons. I really enjoyed his company and was fascinated with his math discussions over dinner at his house. Another person that was particularly interesting was one of the people that worked for me. He had built his own battery powered, ecological proper, Carman-Ghia automobile. It was years ahead of anyone else. Moreover, he actually used it to commute from his home to the university.

Each week end I would drive back to Boulder and spend two days with Merrill and the Children. However one week end when I drove back to Boulder Merrill met me at the door and said "You are out of here, I want you gone right now!". She had done it again, with no employers to contaminate she had to take alternate steps! It was the end of the marriage! I was terribly upset and I thought that insanity has raised it's ugly head for the last time! What an error I made!

I moved everything of mine out of the house and to a 'rent a locker'. I quit my position at Wyoming, and in a state of incredulous shock, I was taken in temporarily by John Johnson, a friend, a radio amateur, and musician that I knew who lived in the area. Forty years later we are still calling each other. Later on I moved in with my sister Dr. Virginia Yeoman who lived near Denver. After the shock wore off it was, once again, time to look for another job.

ALASKA AND THE OIL RUSH

THE TIME WAS 1975 and times were pretty tough for me. My friend John Johnson had taken me in for a while, but soon I moved in with my sister and brother in law, Virginia and Bill Yeoman, down south in Denver, Colorado. They had a house near the Denver airport and you could easily hear the planes making their final approach to the east bound runway because they flew directly over their house. My sister made a room for me in the basement and fed me too. But all the time I was also out looking for work. One hot lead seemed to be doing electronic work for the State, but it was highly political, and pay-offs appeared in order. This went against my grain and thus the job never developed.

One day there was an advertisement in the Denver paper that SCA Corporation was going to be in town interviewing for jobs in Alaska. I just couldn't resist going down for an interview as it sounded exciting. Several men were in Denver from Alaska to find electronic engineers, who had satellite communications knowledge and ability, to help set up a satellite telephone communications system throughout the immense, and almost road less state. At the time there was an oil boom at Prudhoe Bay on the Arctic Ocean and the oil companies were building a pipe line all the way from the north coast across to Valdez, Alaska on the Pacific Ocean, to transport oil to the "lower 48 states" of the U.S. At any rate I went in for the interview and answered a lot of questions about radio communications, transmitters, receivers, and satellites. Naturally, since I had already built the first U.S. satellites and built a lot of transmitters it was easy to answer all their questions.

The interviewers wanted me to go up to Alaska right away and see how the job would actually suit me, and it also would be to allow the men in their office in Anchorage, Alaska a chance to see what they thought of me. This was just a test run, however, and if everything was okay then they would then make an actual job offer. This potential job really brought me out of the doldrums. More than that they suggested that I should take my wife, if I had one, to let her see Alaska too.

Alaska was the land where my Grandfather and Grandmother Cardoza had lived back in the days of the Gold Rush about 1904. They had travelled all over the Canadian Yukon Territory and then down the Yukon River to it's mouth and by boat up to Nome, Alaska on the Seward Peninsula. They lived at Nome for a while until Grandmother became pregnant with my mother, when they sailed south again for the main United States. Grandfather subsequently wrote a book called "Wolf the Storm Leader" about dog teams in Alaska. He had also been actually involved with an epic dog team trip taking a letter 9000 miles, all the way from Nome, Alaska to Wayne Welch in the White House in Washington, D.C. about 1905. So I had a lot of personal interest in going to the arctic, a land I had heard so much about as a child.

At this point I perhaps made a big mistake by calling my paranoid wife Merrill and telling her that "I have a job offer in Alaska, and they want to bring both of us up North to see if we like it". I also told her "It will be an all expenses paid trip, and we can also visit Hawaii on the way back!". My enthusiasm was bursting out I am afraid. She agreed and curbed her venom towards me, at least for the time being. We got on board an aeroplane in Denver and flew via Alaska Airlines to Seattle, Washington, and then on up to Anchorage, Alaska.

Up in Anchorage things also went well at the interview. I had the good sense to avoid letting Merrill meet any of the SCA people. I remember at that time they had a bustling office in a single story office building in the down town area of the city. There were people and cars everywhere and office space was said to be nearly impossible to find then due to the oil boom. The managers approved of me and made me a job offer for wages that sounded very good, particularly after being on university pay rolls, and also after being out of a job for some time. Naturally I accepted.

From Alaska we took an Alaska Airline flight across the Pacific Ocean to Hawaii and landed at main airport at Honolulu on the island of Oahu. From here we flew over to the "big island" and landed at Hilo, Hawaii. We stayed in a condo and traveled around the island sightseeing. To me the most exciting thing was going up on the great active volcano called Mauna Loa and looking down into the great gaping crater filled with still warm lava. While I was looking over the edge there came an enormous rumble of an amplitude that was simply awe inspiring. Frankly it seemed sort of like God speaking, something that is hard to forget.

Years later I had the chance to be close to several other volcanoes when they erupted and my impression of this awesome geologic activity has only been strengthened if anything. The rumble of a volcano, or an earthquake, is certainly something beyond any normal rational human experience, and I can understand why people have been so overcome by their awesome power throughout the long history of man.

The house on top of the mountain near Boulder, Colorado was immediately sold to a radio amateur who just happened to hear me say on the radio that it was for sale. Since it was the ideal radio location he was very excited to get the house. The house cost me about $32,000. dollars in those days to build, but it sold for much more as I remember. So when we went to Alaska we had some money in the bank to buy another home.

The non flying trip to the North was by taking our two trucks to Seattle and loading them on a large Alaska car ferry which was going up the "inland passage" of the Pacific Ocean to Hanes, Alaska. This was a fascinating and interesting trip of several days through the fjords of British Columbia and the lower pan handle of Alaska. We finally arrived at Hanes, Alaska in mid winter, and I remember we spent the first night sleeping in the back of the truck with our little charcoal stove for heat. At least no one froze. The next day we took off for the border of Canada where we would travel for quite a while before we could re-enter Alaska.

This was the land of endless ice and snow. We went up hill for many miles before we came to the Canadian border crossing. Here we were inspected by a man with a big fir Mounty hat, right out of an old movie, who made quite an impression on me. Both our vehicles passed and were allowed into Canada, even with a couple of pistols which were sealed in plastic containers by the officials. As we climbed higher into the interior of the Yukon Territory there was less snow and deeper cold than on the coast. My son Rob-Tom was driving one of the trucks and I was driving the other over the miles and miles of hard frozen dirt roads.

Driving the arctic in the winter was a different experience. Roads were fairly clear of snow and ice but rough and full of so called "wash boards" in many places. It was difficult to go more than about 40 miles per hour, but never the less we were passed by many cars headed north at much greater speeds. Many of the cars in those days carried one, two, or even three, spare tires on their roofs. They needed them too as we could see hundreds of blown tires along the roadsides sticking out of the snow. Every time I stopped I would look at any nearby tires to see why they were abandoned. It was always the same failure, the side walls had blown out. High speed over the extremely rough roads was the devil for tires. Today much of this problem has improved because most of the roads are more smooth.

Rob-Tom had a strange problem along the road in Canada. He was several miles ahead of me but he stopped. As we caught up with him I found him shaking and nervous with a fist size hole completely through his wind shield. He told me that a passing truck had a rock caught between it's dual wheels and this rock was thrown through his wind shield. I had to agree with him completely that it was just plain luck he didn't get hurt. In any case we were able to patch things up temporally and continue on.

At long last we re-entered the Alaska border from Canada and continued on down paved roads to Anchorage. Here we were able to locate a motel to live in until we could find a house. In the mean time I had to check in with SCA and start working.

Finding a house during oil and pipeline economic boom days was a real trick. We found a relatively primitive house for sale on "the hillside" of Anchorage. We put some money down on condition that the house would pass some basic livability tests, like a useable septic system, and well. The house owner was a crusty old codger Alaskan who took the money but steadfastly refused to do the tests

I had required. One day we went down to the bank that was to be the money lender for the house to discuss the problems I had with the old fellow. Here again he refused to return any down payment, or do any of the agreed tests. Merrill started screaming at him at the top of her voice and disturbed the entire bank. People all stared in our direction, and some started running to who knows where. Finally the old man knowingly said "I give up, here is your money back, the woman is crazy."

After the false start in buying a home we at least had our $5,000. dollars back, and were ready to look for another house. This time someone's bad luck was our good luck, in those boom days in Anchorage. We found a home for sale where the owner had just been killed in a car wreck in Valdez, Alaska. The house was newly built and almost finished. Again it was up on the "hill side" of Anchorage. This was a nice two story house on a dirt road some miles south east of down town Anchorage. It was a permafrost area, but I knew nothing of that in those days. We put our money down and all the essential tests went off okay. The bank approved our loan. Now we had a place to live, all four of us moved in, happy to have a liveable home at last.

One of the good things about the new house was that it had a very good bath tub and a good supply of warm water. After a cold day outside in the Arctic it was good to be able to lie back in that tub full of warm water and soak. Only problem with that was that Alaska had the largest earth quake in North America only ten years previously. It was rated as a 9 plus, a world record, on the logarithmic earthquake scale, near the very top of any conceivable earthquake. The earth around Anchorage was still quaking, and continues to quake even as this is being written. It seemed that every time I would get into the tub for some good warm relaxation there would be another earthquake! It would always startle me out of my reverie instantly.

Down at my SCA office there was always plenty of work to do. We were setting up satellite earth stations right and left. Mostly these were four and a half meter diameter parabolic antennas with transmitter-receiver systems that would transmit via a very high geostationary satellite to a ground based master station thousands of miles away, and from there into the main United States telephone and television wire system. This was all new technology in those days and we were always learning better ways to design stations for operation in very remote and primitive arctic locations. Many of our Indian and Eskimo bush sites had very little electricity and had never before had they real telephones, or contact, to the "outside" world. Most locations had almost no outside roads and very minimal bush airports. In those days some transportation was even still done by dog sled. Indeed I remember seeing many of them from an airplane window while travelling along above the winter river ice.

My first Alaska office was on a place called Government Hill since it was one of the first places occupied by the U.S. Government during the founding of Anchorage back about 1915. This was on the north side of Ship Creek, a shallow twenty foot wide stream dividing the portion of the city, where the Air Force now makes their home, and the civilian portions of the city to the south. The office was just outside of the gates of Elmendorf Air Force Base in a crowded one story telephone office building, that apparently had successfully survived the big earth quake of 1964, even though the grade school down the street had collapsed. From this headquarters I was assigned various projects all over the immense state of Alaska.

One important project was to design a specialized satellite earth station up north of Fairbanks at the U.S. Government's Gilmore Creek satellite tracking station near the village of Fox. I was allowed a great deal of latitude and built the station with a large parabolic dish antenna about 7 ½ meters in diameter. Adjacent I built a well insulated electronics building. I also had cables running out to various government buildings in the complex, some as far away as a half mile.

Fascinating things happened during the construction. First was that I had to have a deep hole dug about eight feet in diameter down to bed rock. This was to be filled with concrete to act as solid mounting for my large parabolic satellite antenna. Word went out locally that I was digging a big hole in the ground, and since it was on prime gold dust soil, many of the local people came out to watch and test our diggings for gold. They were there especially on the day we finally hit bed rock. Since it was a well known local legend that just above bed rock was always a layer of nearly solid gold dust, we had quite a crowd. Well we unfortunately we didn't hit any big gold, but there were still people who were nearly breathless until they could see the bottom of that hole, and that it was not yellow.

Later I had hired a man with a back hoe and small tractor to dig a very narrow wire ditch from my instrument building up to another government building where there was a 30 meter diameter monster deep space antenna. The plan was to pipe the deep space radio signals via my earth station directly down to Washington, D.C.

At this time Alaska was largely controlled by the all powerful Federated Union under a local Alaskan Federated big boss. At the time almost anyone working in Alaska except a few engineers were forced to join the Federated Union. This was not just truck drivers by any means, but even medical doctors, nurses, ditch diggers, and electronic technicians, it was near total control. The Big Union Boss heard of my little digging project, well after it's completion, and one day I received a private note from him on small blue, personal note paper, saying "I have determined that your digging a ditch was really a Federated project and you owe me $7,000. dollars." Well we paid him the money rather than have union problems.

Working in the Fairbanks area was exciting in those days since it was the base for the massive North Slope oil pipe line construction. There were jobs for anyone, doing almost anything necessary on a pipe line, and at fantastic wages. Money flowed like water. In my hotel I remember seeing people five deep at the bar, and people in the back waving $1000. Dollar bills in the air to attract bar tender attention. One place I was at, a man yelled "drinks for every union member in the house", and there were plenty. Prostitution was rampant and I often got fliers on my car window advertising specific remarkable services that the friendly girls would provide for me, if I would only call the number on the ad. I saved some of these, but they seem to have wandered away over the years. One of my friends worked at the Fairbanks telegraph office and he told me that one of the independent girls would send fifteen to eighteen thousand dollars home to Tennessee every two weeks! Money flowed like water.

A most scientifically interesting thing also happened while having dinner with a few of my associates in Fairbanks. One man at our table apparently had the same excess of male sex pheromones that I had seen in Louisiana years earlier. He had just flown in from Nome, so he knew no one. In spite of his newness at the hotel, and the great excess of free men, the serving girls kept drifting over to our table and clustered around this one man. He had quite a time fighting them off. There was something about him that just caused nearby women to loose all rational conduct in his presence and throw themselves at him. Later on he told me that it was that way everywhere he went. This was my second confirmation that men do produce a non odorous, but extremely powerful and stinkless scent, or pheromone, that very truly attracts women beyond their ability to rationally control, and that some men have a whole lot more of it than others. Ah, now if I could just buy some of that real male pheromones in a bottle!

Another project at this time was to bring up to date television to the people of Alaska. In those days all television was on video tape put on board the leisurely freight aeroplanes headed for Anchorage. Occasionally the news tapes would be put on faster Alaska Air Lines passenger planes from Seattle, but even here there was no special hurry. Mostly ordinary programs took two weeks to get to Alaska, and even hot news was a day or so behind the actual events. I searched for ways to speed things up and found some possibilities up at Talkeetna, Alaska, a long distance north of Anchorage.

In the days of the Cold War with Russia it was determined that any major satellite earth stations should be at least 100 miles away from any population center to protect the communications system from atomic bombs. Thus when the U.S. Government had a new satellite communications system designed for Alaska it was done by the only official government sponsored corporation for this type of work. The Spacecom Corporation located near Washington D.C. preferred to have the main station built at Talkeetna, Alaska roughly 100 miles north of Alaska's biggest city, Anchorage. This satellite system was to replace the very marginal existing military tropospheric scatter communications system. This old system was a super power "over the horizon" microwave network running through Canada down to the U.S. It used irregularities in the earth's atmosphere to relay signals via monster antennas from one location to another in an unreliable chain. The new satellite signals used by Spacecom were piped from Talkeetna back down to Anchorage by a conventional telephone type microwave radio system so you could at long last call directly from the city to any place in the lower 48 states by a clean sounding telephone link. Another conventional micro wave radio system also paralleled the highway north to Fairbanks, so people there could also call "outside". The Spacecom system was purchased by SCA as Spacecom's governmental charter said that they were limited to communications going outside the United States. SCA had other ideas about how to do things.

I found ways to get TV video signals from the East Coast of the U.S. onto the satellite and from there to the Talkeetna earth station. We contracted for all the programs we could get free, or nearly free, from the SCA earth station near New York City. Mostly this was news and some sports programs. This type of arctic TV broadcasting had only been done in Canada up to this time and I followed as much of the Canadian prototype as was reasonable. Of course satellite broadcasting was becoming immensely popular in the main portion of the U.S. and in particular explicit sex programming was really pushing some people to put money into home satellite earth stations. Thus after originally installing the satellite TV equipment at Talkeetna I went out to the station one day, a week later, and found the entire crew standing in front of a TV monitor with their mouths open. They had discovered that the XXX rated sex channel could indeed be received perfectly with their huge 30 meter satellite dish. No one else in Alaska could see this spicy stuff in those days, and the station crew was first. Consequently no work was done at the Talkeetna earth station for some time!

Back in Anchorage I arranged for the local television stations to set up micro wave radio links from each of their studios over to our main telephone building at Government Hill. At long last the City could view same day television of the kind that people in the lower 48 states had seen for years over the existing transcontinental microwave link system. In Alaska it was revolutionary to see the news the same day it happened. After doing this I wanted to expand. I knew that we had a microwave phone link system that went from Anchorage to Fairbanks some 350 miles north which might be used to carry the TV programs up to Fairbanks. At every microwave station along the highway there was a duplicate back-up transmitter. What I planned to do was pipe the video from Talkeetna up to Fairbanks on this redundant microwave system, even though it was really designed only for telephones. Remarkably it worked fairly well, except the TV in Fairbanks was only in black and white due to the narrow bandwidth of the telephone back-up system that I was forced to use. Converting this system to color was an interesting project too. I got free information from the Tektronics Corporation on how to use their oscilloscopes to increase our microwave system bandwidth. Luckily we had plenty of their best oscilloscopes. Their brochures were distributed to all the technicians along the highway to Fairbanks. With a little tweaking of the intermediate frequency amplifiers in each relay station, suddenly the existing telephone microwave station became a television compatible microwave station. Abruptly Fairbanks had color television much to the surprise and delight of the TV stations engineers, and especially the public.

Up north on the Arctic Ocean my company was installing a satellite earth station at Point Barrow, the northern most town in the United States. This remote Eskimo village is along the ocean coast some 200 miles to the west of the oil fields at Prudhoe Bay and south of the North Pole. All of the excitement of finding oil in this area was new and different to the natives living here. Their world had been relatively unaffected by other civilizations for perhaps 5000 years. Now it was time for change, a radical change. There would be television and telephones to replace the old military short wave radio that was used only in emergency. Now Articom would put in an earth station and people could have home telephones and see TV from "outside".

The management of Articom were not people who had grown up in Alaska and they had little real idea of the differences in native peoples and their antagonisms toward each other. To our bosses all races were all pretty much the same; "You know Indians, Eskimos, they are all about the same, yes?" Consequently they found an engineer at our office in Anchorage who had an Indian wife, and sent them both to Point Barrow to live and install the new satellite earth station. Shortly the engineer returned and he let the company management know that he was definitely not wanted at Point Barrow, and especially his Indian wife was not wanted.

I remember talking to this man and he said "we are not wanted up there, we had to leave and come back here it wasn't safe up there". The management in Anchorage recognized the trouble, in their "outside Alaska" way, and figured out how they would solve this little dilemma. They would send our one Black engineer up there. The logic seemed to be; 'All minorities are pretty much the same therefore this should solve this little race problem'. Well I remember talking to this engineer as he landed back in Anchorage. His comments to me were pitiful: "I got off the airplane and the people kept shouting 'Honky go home, Honky go home, Honky go home'. I have never been called a Honky before, so I came back." You should know that in those days the term 'Honky' was a Black insult exclusively reserved for whites in the lower 48 states of the U.S. Well for quite a while there was no engineer at all at Point Barrow and they had endless technical problems. At least I could see a slight bit of twisted humor in this racial headache and the failed attempted solution.

One more problem was maintaining a satellite station in the extreme north without qualified humans to look after the often unknown problems of operating in the arctic cold. Consequently the extremely large battery bank that ran our station was run down to the worst possible "dead battery" condition, after which the electric generator would not start. This means that perhaps hundreds of gallons of battery acid turned to ice mush and later froze solid breaking the batteries open. Without electricity all automated satellite systems quit running and the broken batteries spread an acid slush all over the floor making a nasty environment when humans finally returned to the building to find out why the telephones quit working.

Being a pilot I just had to have an aeroplane to fly around Alaska. I can't remember where I found it but I bought a Beech model A23 low wing aeroplane. This was a remarkable in certain ways. It had an extra control to retract the landing gear, but it really had no retractable landing gear! It was a special advanced practice plane for pilots transitioning to retractable gear aircraft. The plane was quite hot for an ordinary Alaska private plane and it cruised along at about 135 miles per hour, maybe even 140. It also landed very hot for a private plane in Alaska on icy runways and would quit flying at perhaps 65 miles per hour or perhaps a shade over that speed, at the legal high limit for such planes. This is not what the manufacturer claimed in the instruction manual, but it is certainly is what it did for me. Most other planes would touch down at perhaps 45 miles per hour while this one needed a lot more speed to make a safe landing, or to make a take off. There was always trouble in the landing patterns at the various airports since I had a hard time avoiding overtaking almost all other slower aircraft in the pattern. The control towers were quite unhappy.

My beech also required a hard surface runway in good condition for normal take-offs and landings. I remember one dark winter evening there was an inch or so of wet snow on the runway at Anchorage's Merrill Field when I took off. It took me the entire mile length of the paved runway to get into the air due to the resistance of the snow slush. My pucker factor reached it's maximum at the end of the runway. I decided right there to tell the control tower that I was returning for a landing. This landing was at least uneventful. However, I also decided that the Beech A23 was not the plane for Alaska and it was time to sell.

With some money in my pocket from the sale of the plane I found another aircraft for sale near Chicago, Illinois. I flew down on a commercial plane and landed at O'Hare airport. One of the other passengers from the north had considerable problems with U.S. Customs. He had been hunting in Canada and had a rifle for which customs insisted they would need to put on extra personnel to allow him to be properly inspected. This would cost the poor fellow several hundred dollars extra. Luckily I had no problems with Customs and departed O'hare. I drove over to the other airport and inspected the 150 horse power Champion 7GCAA aeroplane that was advertised and found it appeared to be in good condition and recently recovered with a good synthetic fabric. This plane had an old fashioned tail wheel rather than a modern nose wheel like my Beech. It also held two people with the pilot sitting in front of his passenger, or his luggage, as the case might be. This appeared to be ideal for Alaska conditions. I made the purchase on the spot.

A front was coming in to the Chicago area at the time I took off. I had prepared a flight plan at the motel the previous night and was ready to go as soon as the deal was closed. The take off was uneventful even though I had never flown this type of plane before. Due to the low clouds I had to fly about 1000 feet above ground level all the way to the Mississippi River. There the wind was so bad that I had to hunt to find an airport with a runway facing into the wind. I remember finding a proper landing strip almost on the river but nearly taking out a runway light due to the plane drifting off the side of the runway. After all I was still getting used to this new aeroplane.

But I was able to refuel after finding someone with a key to the gas pump. It was not a very big airport.

After take-off I headed for Minnesota and North Dakota. Flying along I noticed the compass went crazy. The engine vibration started to cause it to simply spin on it's support pins. I had no idea of which way I was going except by following the highways and rivers. Luckily I was an old professional navigator and was able to fly without a compass, but a spinning compass was definitely not my favorite way to navigate. Thus I found a larger airport near the Canadian border and landed. Here I was able to purchase a new compass for the plane. With it installed the whole world seemed better and flying took on a new meaning of joy.

Flying north I landed at Regina to pass Canadian Customs. As usual they were very pleasant and helpful. It took a very short time for the inspection and off I went again to the North West. The time was mid winter and I was flying by way of Calgary and Edmonton into the mountains and then up the Alaska Highway. Flying the Highway was just in case of engine trouble I would have somewhere to land where there would be people and at least a remote possibility of rescue.

The ceiling came lower and lower as I approached the mountains. Actually visibility was terrible and marginal for flight but there was no choice but to go forward. At one point I thought I was near my target airport and I called them on the radio to say I would be landing. A few minutes later I found that the river I was following was much farther away than anticipated probably due to the really bad visibility. It took another thirty minutes to get to the airport and I decided that I would stay there until the sky cleared up and I could enter the mountains safely.

In Fort Nelson I remember being picked up at the airport by a local taxi driven by a woman about seventy years old. The first thing she said was very emphatic, "I want you to know I am not a taxi driver, but I am really a Bull Cook for a lumber camp!" After this admission we had quite a good discussion about lumber camps and cooks. She took me to a local motel that had a Chinese restaurant just down the street. I can remember the French speaking woman at the motel desk had little business at that time of year and so we started a friendly conversation, in English. I told her I was part Scott and part

French, and with that background I should run for political office in Canada. She laughed and said "With that background every one will be mad at you!" My political aspirations were dashed.

It was necessary to wait several days there while the weather cleared up. The Chinese restaurant down the street served up some really unique food. Their meat had small back bones about the size of a cat's backbone, and I suspected that was exactly what it was. Somehow I just couldn't get very excited over their menu. Lucky that soon the weather cleared up and I was able to take off again and head for a slot visible in the mountain wall ahead with the descriptive name on the map of "Canyon of the Drowned". I remember there were no roads to follow or emergency landing sites in the area, nothing but rock walls and a relatively high pucker factor. After a while I was able to relax a bit when I picked up the Alaska Highway beneath me and I headed on west toward Alaska.

It was fascinating country to fly over at low altitudes. You could see that there had been some colossal rains in the past that had stripped all the vegetation from large parts of the mountains and washed rocks into large alluvial fans below me. Eventually I flew over twisted eskers, or the remains of rivers that had flowed underneath the massive glaciers that once covered all this land. The snake like rock mounds continued for miles generally along my path. Eventually I found Whitehorse in the Yukon Territory and landed on their good paved runway. The airport was down in a deep river valley such that looking out of the plane I could see it's walls passing beside the plane on my final approach. At Whitehorse it was possible to park the plane and walk up hill only a short way to a motel near the airport and get some rest.

The next day I had to fly to the U.S. border airport and officially enter the United States again. Here the Customs officer led me into a conference room and made me sit down and listen to about a half hour speech apologizing for the past sins of the previous U.S. customs people. They had been caught in a familiar corrupt operation where they would hold up passing pilots saying that they needed more personnel to check out his plane, but that they could hire the necessary people if the pilot would just give them a few hundred dollars more. Naturally after waiting for many hours in arctic cold the hapless pilots, or his passengers, would often "find" some extra cash to "hire" the "necessary" assistants. I had seen similar custom scams in the past so I knew exactly what he was talking about. Apparently after the fraud was exposed the agents involved were removed, but the new agents were forced to apologize to every pilot passing through their airport.

On the way down to Anchorage from the border I remember flying over endless mountain ridges that appeared to be almost like giant waves in the ocean. Following the road down between the mountains toward Anchorage, suddenly near Palmer, Alaska my air speed indicator went up and up and up until it said I was flying at more than 200 miles per hour, rather than the proper 125 miles per hour I had been doing up to this time. It is surprising how much I depended on that wonderful little air speed instrument for proper control of the plane. I knew that the engine revolutions had not changed, so I would have to depend on them to be an indicator of the real speed I was flying. This would be especially important on the final approach to landing in Anchorage. It was not a good speed indicator, but it was the best I could do at this time. Everything worked out alright, and I made an uneventful landing at Merrill Field in Anchorage. The problem was found to be that the pipe going to the air speed indicator somehow became full of ice.

Back at my home base my company, Articom, had plenty of work for me, and there were still plenty of strange adventures to be had. One of my friends at work was from Holland but he had learned English working in a winery in Georgia. Thus he spoke, not with a Dutch accent, but with a very good southern U.S. accent. He also had built his own simple, rectangular, flat bottomed boat from pieces of plywood. I think the basic design was drawn from a cardboard box. He invited me, and one of the other engineers, to go fishing in the middle of Cook Inlet, a very large ocean fjord extending from the Pacific Ocean up to Anchorage. We launched his boat somewhere near Clam Gulch, Alaska about half way between the open Pacific Ocean and Anchorage. Here the inlet is about 30 miles wide and we headed right out to the middle in his frail plywood boat shaped like a box. We anchored in the middle and threw out our halibut fishing lures. The local tidal current was tremendously strong due to Cook Inlet having the world's second largest tides. As the tide slowly changed direction, the current slackened, and we started catching halibut, a big strong flat fish. They would be brought on board and then they would flail about strongly seemingly trying to bash the plywood bottom out of the boat so they could return to the sea. Somehow we survived a number of these fishing trips without losing the bottom of the boat.

Hunting too was great sport in Alaska. One of my buddies wanted to go caribou hunting so I looked over the topographic maps to try to identify a place we could be sure to get a caribou. I found what looked good in a small body of water called Watana Lake. To get there we went to Lake Grege where we found a man with a Cessna 206 rental plane service on floats that could get us back into the remote lake. We put our camping goods, fishing rods, and rifles on board and headed out. Landing at the lake we found there were utterly no roads any where in the vicinity, but there was one rustic cabin on the lake. Taxing the plane about we found a good camp site a mile south where the sound of the plane scared off a grizzly bear as we pulled ashore. The pilot promised to return in a few days and pick us up, then he gave his plane the gun and departed.

With our small tent set up we decided to try some fishing and found it astoundingly good. We were pulling in good sized lake trout with each cast of our lures. We put each fish back carefully so they would live for another wide eyed fisherman. Then we had an occurrence that could only happen in a remote Alaskan place. Two men with a shot gun came walking up to our camp. We asked where they came from and they said they had come up the Susitina River but mostly they had a hard time talking in English. I could hear them talking in German and understood enough to know that they had stolen a boat and come up the river until it ran out of fuel. Now they appeared to have broken into the nearby cabin and stolen guns and provisions. It appeared that they had been stealing their way around the world from Hamburg, Germany. Now with everyone's guns in hand I thought we should sleep very lightly that night. We kept our rifles loaded and right at hand, but we never saw the two men again. My partner had an Olympic class snore that I am sure scared off the bad men, and our grizzly bears too.

The next day we went out on the nearby hillsides looking for signs of caribou and we found plenty. The "boo" as they were called locally had a trail around the end of the nearby mountain between it and the lake. Pretty soon a few "boo" came down the path and we both took one with easy rifle shots. Then the work of cleaning and dressing the meat started. We had to get everything down to a size that would fit on the plane going back to Lake Grege. The pilot returned but with a Piper Super Cub on floats, a much smaller plane. He said he would take us one at a time along with our game and camping gear. The plane was tremendously overloaded in the way Alaskans call "Alaska gross". Such planes on floats will run along the lake at full speed and see if they can get airborne. If they don't get into the air by the end of the lake the pilot will turn around and take some of the goods out of the plane and try again until he can get it flying. Well my flight made it up into the air the first time but it was clearly overloaded as there seemed to be problems controlling the plane. Very carefully we flew over another small lake where the pilot said the past President of the United States, Jimmy Carter, liked to fish. Eventually both of us hunters and our "boo" made it safely back to our vehicles at Lake Grege and then back to Anchorage.

Flying in my "Champ" was a way to see some of the more remote parts of Alaska, and also to view some places not far from Anchorage which were seldom visited by anyone. For example I decided that I would try to land anywhere that I thought there was a reasonable chance of making a good landing. Probably this is something that was really stupid, but I figured that I needed some real adventures while I was living on the "last frontier" as they called Alaska. Oil wells had been drilled on the west side of Cook Inlet and they had put in some primitive dirt roads from the Indian village of Tyonek. These roads were only traveled when it was necessary to service a remote oil well. Since they had no power or telephone lines beside the roads I decided to land on some of them. It took all my piloting skill to make the landings since the roads were just two tire tracks exactly the width of my landing gear, but I did make it okay. Another dumb landing was at the foot of Knik glacier. I could see that there was little here except gravel brought down and deposited by the glacier, but it did have lots of dry stream channels wandering through it. By cruising back and forth over the gravel at about a five foot altitude a number of times at a hundred miles and hour I finally lined up an area without ditches across it. I set up for a landing and noticed that the cold air from off the glacier ice was flowing exactly opposite of the air a hundred feet higher. I had to go back and recalculate my landing, but I somehow did make it safely. I had time to walk about in an area seldom visited by anyone else.

Occasionally I would fly up to my work at Fairbanks. This meant flying past the largest mountain in North America, Mt. McKinley or Denali as it is called today. The height was 21,000 feet, or 6,400 meters. Winds in this area were greatly controlled by the massive mountain, and it was necessary to fly up a broad canyon then through a narrow embrasure in the mountains, to get to the north side and then down another canyon out onto the relatively flat land around Fairbanks. Once flying down this canyon from the north my rate of climb gage said I was falling at more than 2000 feet per minute. I had to turn around and return to Fairbanks. I called the Federal Aviation Administration on the plane's radio and told them about the problem with the high sink rate by Denali mountain. A minute later I heard them warning all other aircraft that the pass was closed due to the high downdrafts.

There was much else about flying in Alaska that was different than other parts of the world. There were almost no gas stations for aircraft and it was necessary to plan flights very carefully. Head winds could cause a plane to run out of gas before arriving at the next airport. Many pilots carried five gallon "Jerry cans" of gas in the back seat rather than passengers. I also tried this, but finding a landing spot to refill the tanks is also a real trick. In the Anchorage area, perhaps within a hundred miles, there are many small home built runways, I would bet a hundred or more. These ordinarily have no services or people anywhere in the vicinity, and worst of all you never have any real knowledge how the surface of the runway was going to treat your plane. I'll bet I landed at a couple of dozen of these micro airports and probably an equal number of river sand bars and such. Occasionally there were slightly larger runways remaining from World War II or from oil exploration activities long since past. For me these were the best places to land and explore. Perhaps this also was the real beginning of my interest in becoming a helicopter pilot.

Back in Anchorage I would take my daughter Dianna to her special high school every day on the way to work. This was a school for children with learning problems, or other difficulties, of one kind or another. However with the full help of her sick mother Dianna "ran away" to Boulder, Colorado. Her mother had filled her full of her own warped psychological problems to the degree she thought she was in a terrible place and in an impossible situation, and she thought she should do what ever her mother suggested, which was at the moment to "run away". In actual fact I put her on the airplane south. She was convinced that she could take care of herself all alone in Boulder and she would have no problems going to high school there and earning an income too. When she arrived she found that her mother's plans were total pure fantasy and that she had to work full time as a waitress to survive, school was out of the question. Eventually she returned to Anchorage and finished her high school there with my help alone.

20

MURDER, ALMOST

DAY BY DAY Merrill was also becoming very much more strange too, dangerously sick! By that time we had twin beds as the compatibility level was zero. One day I walked into the bedroom in stocking feet and as I approached my bed I stepped on many pins that just happened to be sticking point up from the carpet. I asked Merrill how all the pins got there and how they all got to be point up. Her answer was that she had been sewing and they just happened to all fall that way. After they had been removed I laid down on the bed and immediately got stabbed by a dozen or so more pins all sticking vertically up through the cover of the bed. I got the same answer from Merrill, she had been sewing there and the pins just fell under the top cover and all happened to fall point up in that location.

But that was not the worst she could do by any sick thinking. One day I was fishing all alone near a remote creek, by the highway, at the head of Cook Inlet. Standing all alone on the treeless mud flats someone took a shot at me. The sound of the bullet passing so close to my ear was deafening! I yelled at the invisible person hiding in the shore line brush 200 yards away to "watch where you are shooting". With this there was another shot, and another, deafeningly close to my ears! It was an assignation attempt! I dove behind a large boulder that was sticking up from the mud flats. And there were more shots in my direction, I counted twenty in all. I laid face down in the mud for perhaps a half hour, and there were no more shots, so very carefully I got up and went toward the place where the shooter had been hiding. I found a number of .223 rifle cartridge cases but no indication of any bottles, cans, or paper targets, or any thing else the shooter might have been firing at, except me. I had been all alone on a vast open mud flat near a stream, a perfect target. I could only think that Merrill had seen my parked car along the road and found the perfect opportunity to kill me at a remote place, without any witnesses.

This was clearly time to move out of the house and into an apartment in Anchorage. It was also time to think about permanently separating from Merrill and moving as far away as possible. Soon Merrill wrote me a remarkable letter about the shooting incident, but reversed all of the facts making herself the alleged pawn, in her customary insane fashion of reversing the truth. I thought, who but the shooter would know all of the facts about the shooting incident, and be able to make up such a cover story. I wondered in my mind how long am I going to last with this psychotic shooter after me? Will it be until she wears her glasses and her aim gets better, or until she finds some other method of murder?

At the time I worked on the top floor of SCA's very large new office building in Anchorage. One day I got a urgent call from the front desk saying that "your wife is here in the lobby with a bunch of pipes screaming and shouting that she wants to 'stick them up your ass', please do something about it!" I went down to the lobby and sure enough there was Merrill screaming lots of obscenities at everyone. There were a number of people there with extremely astonished looks on their faces, and Merrill was indeed waving a very large section of an antenna mast about violently. I took the mast from her and went out the back door with it, throwing it in the building trash pile, and I yelled to the guard that there was an insane woman in the lobby, and kept on going. It was time to find another job a long way away! I had enough of insanity if I wanted to live!

I had a couple of weeks of vacation saved up so I told Greg Morgen, my boss at SCA, that I would like to take a vacation. My plan was to find another job at a safe distance from Merrill, perhaps somewhere not in Alaska. The Spacecom Company that had put the original satellite earth stations into Alaska was advertising for engineers 9000 miles away in Washington D.C. and this looked extremely enticing. I contacted them and they were interested in me.

All I needed to do now was an interview. My plan was that if I landed the job I would call Greg and tell him why I could not come back to work for SCA. It was a matter of life or death for me to disappear.

About the same time one of my divorced Friends, Emma, had a personal disaster happen. Two of her sons were attending West Point Military Academy run by the United States Army. The younger son was in a boxing match and his opponent gave him a fatal punch to the head which caused a brain hemorrhage. It was a disaster for her, and even worse, since she had to tell the hospital to turn off his life support equipment. To add to the blow her house was robbed, during her son's funeral.

As high school aged children Emma and I had been quite close buddies. We had seen each other fairly frequently and often exchanged rather passionate letters. Since she was now living with another relative in Washington D.C. I thought I should call on her while I was making the Spacecom interview and give her my condolences over the loss of her son. Somehow it turned out to be very much more than that.

The Spacecom interview went smoothly and I was hired to be an engineer designing satellite earth station equipment for their world wide network of stations. I was to work in a laboratory just north of Washington's main beltway under former Army General Peter North. The work was something that was perfectly suitable for me, the kind of thing I had plenty of experience doing. More than that my people would be designing and building equipment for some of the world's largest and most complex international earth stations in countries like Australia, Japan, Italy, Brazil, and about two hundred other countries.

With a good stable job at last and a long way from danger, times seemed much better for me. Also Emma and I decided, as buddies, to buy a house together, one just north of the Washington belt way. It was a good place with a large apple tree in the back yard, a spacious studio adjacent to the house, and plenty of room. We moved in along with Emma's youngest son who was of college age but not yet attending college. Emma soon got a job as a legal secretary with a law firm in the Washington area. There were various other Friends in the area too, so we were kept busy both socially and with work. My running was over.

21

MORE "SPACY" THINGS

Well Washington, D.C. seemed a good place to live. Just outside of the Beltway in Bethesda was a bit noisy, except at 3 AM on Sunday morning when the traffic slowed down a bit. Emma and I enjoyed living together in the Big City where we both had good jobs. I was an engineer for Spacecom and in charge of building test equipment for their world wide satellite earth station complex. It had much to do with space.

Emma also got a job as a legal secretary at one of the nation's largest law firms in down town Washington. Her youngest son, one her three, lived with us, and he was a bit of a problem to me. He was convinced by "friends" that he was a sexual Liberal. In Washington he found lots of established Liberals to keep him going in that mode. I found out that "they" had an itching to propagandize young people to attempt to convince them that they too are sexual Liberals too, and more over should have sex with them. Very clever propaganda it is too. Anyway they tend to really enjoy the company of hansom young boys like Emma's son, and he was soon wearing a radio call device on his belt to keep liberal hormones happy. He got calls day and night.

If you wonder about marriage, well Emma's father insisted, very strongly, that if we were going to live together we must get married. I looked into cousins getting married and found it was legal in Maryland, and we were in Maryland. So we did get legally married.

And if you wonder if we slept in the same bed, yes we did, and it was very good. She was a good bed partner, not a drop of insanity.

My work was mostly outside the Beltway in a laboratory located a few miles north of the city. We produced some very complex racks of electronic hardware to test the quality of signals into countries all over the world. I would manage both, design and construction of this hardware. In addition I also would arrange for engineers to be sent with it to help in the installation in some of the hundred plus countries. It was fun to send people off to places like the bush in Australia and hear their comments on their return. One man made several trips to Italy where he got in a traffic accident and caused me all sorts of trouble. But in the long run most things worked quite well.

There were several radio hams who worked for me. Being one myself gave us a reason to sit around the lunch table and trade stories about our own adventures talking to other continents and such. One of the fellows enjoyed the very high frequency (VHF) bands. Consequently I added a special antenna to my airplane for this frequency and flew him and one of his sons about the area at high altitude. They made quite remarkable radio contacts from the plane too.

From time to time Spacecom had me do other special projects for them. One was to help with the marine satellite system development. This was the beginning of using satellites for communications to ships, but today it is the accepted way of communication for all large ships. My experience as a ship board radio officer using a telegraph key and low frequencies helped my acceptance by the marine people a bit. However, this was a new beginning for ship board communications in 1980 and it was a very good beginning with only a few serious problems.

22

VOICE OF AMERICA

ALL OF MY trips over seas seemed to call to me. One of my Washington friends told one of branches of the CIA that I would be a good person for a job in Iraq. So I got a phone call from a man who was very insistent that I come and see him in one of the Washington suburbs. He had a job that was just the thing for me, and he said he had already heard all about me from some of my friends.

He gave me no opportunity to say no, and gave me the address. So I got in the car and went down to the location I had been given. It was a long, long, two story building with a large parking lot in front. Remarkably there were only two cars in the parking lot on this a normal work day. I went to the very ordinary looking front door and rang the bell. After a minute or so a tall, dark haired woman dressed in a black leather suit answered the door. She asked for my name, I gave it, and she said "follow me".

I was led up stairs to a large office and met a man there who gave me a few of the details of the proposed job. He said they had an excellent position for me assisting one of the Middle East's top leaders in Iran, and he thought it would be a perfect job for me. He didn't know that I had just read a number of CIA reports of the situations in the Middle East and I said that "no I don't think I want to take your job there". With that he switched to another job he had in Lebanon, again he said "perfect for you". Now that was another place where the CIA had just identified some twenty different factions all fighting each other. Again my answer was "sorry but no thanks". The man had a huge map of Alaska on the wall of his office for some unknown reason, so I pointed at it and said "that is where I want to go!"

Well mutually we decided to part company and to forget the Middle East spy work. Alaska didn't make any hit with him either. As we parted I asked if he was with the CIA and got nothing but a hand shake. Some information, some how, "leaked" to certain people in Washington.

Later I got another call and was asked to meet a man who had been head of the "Voice of America", or VoA. They are now closely allied to the State Department and to the CIA. Remarkably the secret meeting was to be at a street corner in down town Washington. I went down and found the man among all the other people walking the side walk. We sat on a park bench with a variety of people walking by, and discussed my experiences around the world with the Department of Defense, and in electronics at Spacecom. After about thirty minutes he said "you sound like VoA could use you and I will tell them so.

A meeting was scheduled at VoA headquarters in a much more formal situation. I was to meet with several PhD's, one at a time, who would analyze my potential value to VoA. Each man gave me the sort of a verbal test, like they give PhD's at the university. There was no question it was stressful. Each man told me that the final decision would be by the one man who was the present head of the VoA organization.

This man seemed to have every one at VoA running scared. They said he copies the methods of the old head of the Federal Bureau of Investigation, Edgar Hoover, and keeps an evidence file on every one he can get evidence on to control. Later on I would indeed inherit his files on people, but his acceptance of me only took a day.

Emma had no comments about me changing jobs. She had already changed jobs herself a couple of times between law firms. Also I suspected there might be more going on as she never wanted me to drive her to her job, but rather let her off invisably around the corner and out of sight of her building. She also was taking courses at the University of Maryland to get a BA degree with an emphasis on writing. Part of that was because I had met a book publisher at the private airport where I kept my plane, and this contact had a lot of potential for publishing a book, and Emma liked to write books.

The first thing that happened when I went to work for the Voice of America was they said "you are going to Switzerland to help out in a meeting we are giving over in Europe". So very shortly I was on a plane with a diplomatic passport in hand on my way to Geneva, Switzerland. Since we would be in the country for some time we rented a second story apartment near Lake Geneva from a Communist college student. First thing I noticed was that the apartment was full of books about Lenin and communism. The next thing I noticed was that the old French I spoke when I was a small child only got the people to laugh at me, and I don't blame them. I must have sounded like I was four years old.

Much of my time was spent at the hall where the Voice of America had a display booth. We answered questions and gave out small pieces of memorabilia about VoA. Much of the time here was spent in talking with people about "things" of interest to the United States. Many of the people I talked with were Communist Russians, and they were a very highly educated class of Communist Russians too. After spending several days talking to them I got the distinct impression that Communist Russia was falling apart internally. The Malia ("charm" in Italian) type of government had burned out in the good old Communist empire.

VoA also happened to have a number of very high power broadcast transmitters stashed away in Switzerland in the city of Baden. This is a northern city where there are hot springs that have been used for baths since the time of the Romans. It is also in the German speaking part of the country and I could get along much better than in the French speaking areas. Consequently I very much enjoyed living in this area. I loved walking down streets where the houses had been built in the year 1200 AD, or perhaps earlier. There were still Roman statues here and there, and my best memory is of a mother telling her little boy what the statues were doing. Many of the people I talked to said "speak English" as they wanted to learn English, but theirs was so bad it was hopeless for me. I felt sorry that I could not do more for them.

While in Switzerland I got to travel a good deal and see much of the country. In addition it was possible to sample the wines, beers, cheeses, and such things. My conclusion was that the Swiss cheeses are excellent, so are their beers, but their wines are not so good. I had sampled plenty of French and German wines are found them excellent, but the Swiss have yet to learn good wine making, at least according to me.

Back in the United States I reported my findings on the real condition of the Communist Russian internal government directly to the President Reagan in the White House. His people in the White House told me that Ronald Reagan went 'dancing' through the building after he got my report. Shortly after this the Berlin Wall fell as I recall, and later the Communist Russian Communist government disintegrated. I feel I had really done something remarkably important by listening carefully to all those intelligent Russians.

Here in the U.S. there was one project after another waiting for me. They knew that I had lots of satellite experience so I was made project manager for a proposed several billion Dollar satellite broadcast station that was to be aimed for broadcasting directly to Russia. This was a huge project with a budget that was more than the entire VoA agency spent in several years. Our VoA leader was very interested in all such "big highly visible projects" and this was certainly one of those.

This would have been a satellite with very large high frequency phased array antenna pointing down at Russia from space, and many other countries. It would shoot through the formidable solar ionized cloud that covers the earth in day light hours by using all sorts of clever means. I could say that it was entirely possible to build such a satellite, but it would have required an act of Congress to supply the vast amount of money necessary, and probably would have changed every aspect of the Voice of America completely. Consequently I killed this project as being very unlikely to ever get funded.

Well there was also an interest in Washington in putting in VoA broadcast stations in Central America. This had a lot to do with the Communist Russian influence in Cuba and Nicaragua, and their continued forceful attempts to take over some of the Caribbean Islands and countries. I got this project because I had already some considerable experience in the Caribbean area, and spoke a few words of Spanish too. First I went to some of the English speaking islands like Antigua, Barbados, Montserrat, St. Lucia, and Grenada, places where I had lived back in my Department of Defense days, places that I knew well.

Grenada has just been invaded by the United States military and freed from Communist Cuban or Communist Russian rule. It was fascinating for me to be able to search the Communist Russian embassy building and find their secrets. Things like a hidden basement full of machine guns and hand grenades, a back yard with buried cases of ammunition, things like that. There were several Communist Russian air planes, like AN-2s, at the small airport on one end of the island. There was a good deal of damage from fighting and I visited their short wave radio station but I worried about remaining booby traps a good deal.

Somehow on Grenada I caught some sort of strange bug. It took me about a month to recover from the booby trap sickness, and I spent some time in Washington, D.C. in the hospital. But everything turned out okay.

On another trip I went down to investigate an existing short wave station on the island of Montserrat. The idea was to broadcast to the entire Caribbean from here to counter the Communist Russian influence. The existing radio station on this island was on the west flank of Mount Soufriere, a very active volcano. Just for fun I went down in the crater of the volcano all alone among the vents of sulfur gas and boiling hot water springs. Later on, shortly after I left, the volcano "went off" and devastated much of the island.

Later on I spent quite a while on the western side of the Caribbean Sea, in the Spanish speaking countries of El Salvador, Honduras, and Guatemala. In addition I spent a while in the English speaking country of Belize setting up a broadcast radio station to cover the various Spanish speaking areas that were under pressure from the Communist Cuban supported revolutionaries.

The station in Belize was quite different from anything else in the Central American area. First the transmitters were rather high powered at 100,000 watts, quit a bit more than the 50,000 watts generally allowable in North America. In addition I had horizontal antennas installed, rather than the normal vertical antennas. This would give more coverage back in the mountains of Central America instead of what could be expected of the local coverage from normal vertical broadcast antennas. Indeed the coverage was very good all the way down to Managua, Nicaragua where the communists controlled the country.

Later I spent quite a while in Honduras where they had a real invasion from the Nicaraguan troops. I was on the front lines and even went in some homes where they were barricaded against the foreign invaders. These places were interesting; every one had loaded fire arms and places for everyone to hide much like the Mexican revolution in my mother's day. Afterward I spent some time talking to news men who had come from the North to get stories, and I gave them plenty. I tried to tell them that the communists wanted U.S. citizens to come down and get killed so that bad things could be blamed on their anti communist foes. However this sort of story was not as popular as they hoped.

In these countries at war I was provided a "bullet proof" armored car and personnel body guards with sub machine guns. Of course there were enough guns to let me have one too, if I ever needed one. We spent quite a bit of time traveling alone through the country and never ran into any one else traveling around like I did due to the wars going on. At night in El Salvador I would hear the shooting start in the evenings and lots of machine guns firing. Later in the day light it would seem to be much quieter. Interestingly I lived in a room adjacent to the leader of the anti communist guerrillas and he was often very nervous, so I was too, back in those days.

Back in Washington, D.C. things were so much different. Living with Emma was peaceful and quiet and she had no idea what was going on outside the U.S. She had her own life, with the lawyers she worked for, her liberal son, and with one of her sisters who was married to a Cypriot economist who also lived in Washington but who had lived long in Brazil and elsewhere.

As for me, I spent my time traveling from country to country. Another place I went was Korea. It was a long air trip from Washington to New York and then non stop to Seoul half way around the world in first class. I went to work at the U.S. Embassy where they offered me lessons in the Korean language while I helped them with our plans and ideas for big radio stations to broadcast to Russia and China.

There was one Army colonel who would rush in to my office early every morning asking "what new ideas do you have today". After I would tell him, I found he would immediately rush off to the ambassadors office and tell him "his ideas" for the day. When I got in to see the ambassador, what I said was old news and worthless.

I also spent much time meeting with Korean officials. It was fascinating to hear the "special voice" that they used only in official conferences. It was a deep and louder voice than normal Korean, very much the same language emphasis used by the Japanese on similar special diplomatic occasions.

One time I went to Pan Mun Jom where the North Korean's met the South Korean's at the "Peace Table" or Peace Treaty point line. I got to see the North Korean propaganda tricks that were being used here, and it was remarkable. At the "Table" one trick or another was used to allow the North to always claim to be superior over the South. For example the North's flag would be made a centimeter higher than the South's. Also a tremendously tall flag pole was erected just outside north of the truce line, and it was probably 200 feet high. In addition a very large fake office building was erected by North Korea that was perhaps 200 feet wide and only 3 feet deep close adjacent to the little Peace Conference Building. It was all for show as I never noticed anyone go in or out of the many doors in this all for "show building". However, there were always North Korean guards with binoculars watching me from the porch of this fake building.

One day I even got to go up to the very front line, perhaps actually into North Korea, where the U.S. maintained a few armed guards. It was scary as we knew that the North Koreans undoubtedly had sniper rifles aimed at our hearts continually. In addition the North Koreans were continually building tunnels under the cease fire line big enough to drive a tank through, or move thousands of troops through, and many had been already found.

Back in Seoul I once got to take my boss's secretary out for dinner once, rather than eat alone in Korean restaurants, or cafeterias. We ordered some of the traditional thin beef slices cooked at the table over a small charcoal burner. This meat was then wrapped up with raw garlic cloves and eaten. The secretary ate quite a number of garlic cloves, probably to keep me at bay. It was quite enjoyable until the next day when we took a taxi and the taxi driver held his nose and said something in Korean about the over powering garlic stink! Of course garlic is the native smell of Korea, we could even smell it at 5000 feet above Seoul when flying over.

Another time I borrowed the U.S. Army general's air plane to fly down to a large island off the south coast of Korea and look for good radio station sites. The plane came with a pilot and co-pilot so I didn't have to do much work. It was fascinating to watch the country side pass below the plane and view the shallow China Sea off our right wing. We also passed a very large atomic power plant along the way which seemed larger than could possibly be necessary here. At last we got to the island off the south coast and flew low over this large piece of land. I was quite disappointed to find that the island was entirely small farms with few good roads and only lots of horses for transportation. It also seemed to have a great lack of power facilities which would be necessary for a large radio station. Consequently we flew back to Seoul.

On another trip to Korea from the U.S. we stopped in Japan for a short visit. During this trip my friends from Washington, D.C. and I spent some time walking around the Japanese country side. It was very educational to learn about the common people in Japan and how they lived and farmed. Quite different than in Korea, and very different from the United States., but very educational.

On the return trip to the U.S. we had to fly on the shortest route which is known as the "Great Circle Route" by old navigators like me. This took us from Tokyo over Alaska and then straight to New York City. Having lived years in Alaska and having some interest in locating a place for a radio station to broadcast to Russia I arranged for a stop-over of a few days. I found a good place or two for radio stations, and published the technical information in the Institute of Electrical and Electronic Engineers journal.

Remarkably I was told in Washington that this was a side trip that was much longer than could be possibly be allowed government people, and I should never do this again. Indeed they made an "iron bound" ruling that absolutely no one could stop in Alaska on a trip to Japan or Korea. However, I could stop in Hawaii on trips to Japan as that was indeed on the direct path to Japan. I was astounded that no one in Washington seemed to know that all air liners flew the Great Circle Route from the U.S. east coast to Japan regularly and normally went over Alaska. Diplomats were only allowed to take a rest stops in Hawaii, but it was fun too.

23

FLIGHT TO ALASKA

BACK HOME IN the state of Maryland I was with my wife Emma. She had been getting along quite well without my help, but with the help of another sister who lived near by. I could also see that all my absences had been hard on her and she was clearly looking for a new boy friend, a lawyer possibly. She worked every day in one of the top law offices in Washington. I got worried when she would not allow me to deliver her to the front door of their office building. I always had to drop her off about a block or two away, out of sight of her building. Naturally I was suspicious that something was going on.

At the same time the CIA was putting pressure on me again to go and work for a well known Muslim religious and political leader in the Near East. They knew I had studied Near Eastern languages and I must have looked good to them. Now I had already also studied the CIA reports on this man's country and all other countries around it. My answer was "NO, NO, NO". Well then they said "let me offer you an alternative job in Beirut. Lebanon". I had just read the CIA report about Lebanon, it said there were many different political factions each fighting each other, and none could untangle them. Once again I said "NO NO NO". I must comment that later on in the year a number of U.S. troops were killed at the same place I had just been asked to go.

I already had lived in Alaska and had a good idea of what to expect way up there. So I looked at a U.S. Government list of engineers wanted to see if they had any appropriate jobs in Alaska, and they did. Being a pilot myself I applied for the position as an engineer with the Federal Aviation Administration, and it came through. I would be designing low frequency aviation radio beacons all over the state, and other similar radio stations. I offered to take Emma with me on a truly long driving trip all the way from Washington, D.C. to Anchorage, Alaska so she could see what it was like in Alaska. It was to be a classic long trip, and she said 'yes I'll go with you'. However, she did not sound very happy about the potential change.

We drove all the way to the Canadian border near North Dakota on the way to Regina, Saskatchewan where we planned to stay the night. The city name totally freaked Emma's sense of propriety. She insisted the name was almost the same as vergina and she could not possibly stay at a place with such a sexual name. So we went on to a near by city with the more docile name of Moose Jaw, Saskatchewan. Then west to Calgary, Alberta, and then north on the excellent road to Edmonton, Alberta where I had some relatives.

From Edmonton it was a fairly short way north west to Grande Prairie, Alberta and the start of the Alaska Highway, which supposedly had been designed by one of my relatives named Thompson. I remember staying at a motel here run by a French Canadian woman who was very friendly and receptive to my few childhood words of French.

On we went north west to Dawson Creek, Fort St. John, and Fort Nelson, British Columbia and the start of some beautiful mountainous country. You could see here that over the century's glaciers had done much to the land to leave their marks. There were many drumlins like those I had grown up with in Syracuse, New York. Most of the roads were unpaved at this date and rough and hard on the car. But soon we were on into towns like Whitehorse, in the Yukon Territory and close to the Alaska border.

We crossed the border of Canada and the United States near Beaver Creek, Yukon Territory and went into Alaska. Here I remember staying in a motel that was apparently made of old trucks. It was not much, but certainly different from anything we had seen so far. From the border we went on down the much better quality Alaska roads to Anchorage.

In Anchorage we found that the Oil Boom was over and there were many buildings available to rent. We got a small apartment on the ground floor of one of the buildings and moved in. I also reported for work at the government agency called the Federal Aviation Administration, or FAA for short.

We went out to the Anchorage airport and I put Emma on the plane for Washington, D.C. She arrived and went back to our most recent house just a few miles north of the Washington beltway at Centerwood, Maryland. Shortly later Emma had one of her sisters move in with her. After this a divorce was started to make it a legal separation.

This divorce brought Emma's minimal legal training to the fore. The first thing I knew was that she was demanding that I pay support for her middle aged liberal son who was now also living with her in Maryland, and who had a forty thousand dollar a year job. But she was aware of all the legal tricks. So I ended paying support for an already well paid person who was not my son at all, and it bugged the heck out of me. But the legal system is flawed even to cousins. And finally we made a full separation and I was at last alone in the Alaskan bush, sort of. Truthfully, I officially lived in the city of Anchorage, and spent much of my life flying about to every other possible part of Alaska.

24

LIFE AS A BUSH RAT

WORKING FOR THE Federal Aviation Administration moved me from one area of Alaska near an airport to another airport area. You must be aware that Alaska has almost no roads and relies largely on airplanes to go from one area to another. Of course the cost of air plane travel is expensive, so many people still travel by dog sled in the winter, and in some areas by traditional native boats in summer.

On a number of occasions I went to small town airports on the Bearing Sea across from Siberia, Russia. It appeared that a number of Communist Russians had migrated eastward to Alaska by small boats from Siberia in the Communist days. Russian was still spoken, and modern Communist Russian at that, in some of the Bearing Sea towns. My Russian teacher from Moscow would have been happy with the dialect along the coast.

Much of my time in bush Alaska was spent designing, or modernizing, low frequency radio beacons. These beacons were still used in Alaska as they had excellent low altitude ranges and could cover the great distances between towns in the bush. I even designed a station for a remote island west of Sitka, Alaska that, the math said, could cover the whole distance from Seattle, Washington up north to Anchorage, Alaska with 2000 watts of transmitter power.

This station was to be built to my specifications using a 2000 watt transmitter. However the technicians doing the building did not order the transmitter needed, but used an old transmitter they just happened to have available. Their transmitter was only 500 watts and would reach only half the distance from Seattle to Anchorage. That was life in Alaska, one did what one could with what was available.

On another occasion I was sent out to a remote island in the Aleutian Island chain called Adak. This island had been a Cold War navy base and had a large airport and facility for navy personnel. However it had just been shut down. Remarkably I was given living quarters in an abandoned officers home, which was very, very good. I spent a while here arranging for an effective low frequency radio beacon. But in the interim the Navy Seals were dynamiting a 1000 foot tall radio tower nearby. I wanted the tower for my use, but I was to late and it went down.

There were other things out there too. Things like atomic bomb storage facilities that were no longer used. Runways for bombers were available, and then there were a herd of wild caribou that had been installed on the island in case of isolation and food shortage during the Cold War. These caribou were all to be killed off as they were said to be "non native" to the island. I never did hear if this arbitrary extinction took place.

Way out on the west end of the Aleutian Chain were some islands that had been conquered by the Japanese during World War Two. These had been reconquered by the United States and a military base built at Kiska. There was still some military activity here similar to Adak. I was flown out here in a long range twin engine plane rented by the FAA. I was allowed to ride in the co-pilot's seat which was fun for an old pilot. This was a flat island with a large Cold War airport that had been down graded to a very quiet, and remote, military facility. It was only a short way to Siberia from here. The places invaded by the Japanese at Adak were visible over the water on a nearby island.

While I was out on the Aleutian Chain I ran into some scientists who had just dug up an European skeleton and who were wondering how in the world an European got out on the remote island chain perhaps a thousand years ago. It would seem that we really don't know every thing about who discovered what.

Another island group I went out to in the Bush was the Pribilof's in the middle of the Bearing Sea. This was a most remarkable place geologically. It was almost flat, but with some large round volcanic craters often filled with water or ice. We drove around the island in a tracked vehicle and visited small FAA sites and could really feel that we were at the end of the earth.

Later I visited the remote Saint Lawrence Island again far out in the Bearing Sea and not far off the coast of Siberia. You could see Siberia from here. We visited the Eskimo towns of Savoonga and Gambell. This last was almost within sight of the Russian city of Providenja. I remember falling off the sled we were traveling on and worrying about being eaten by wandering Polar Bears, which was a real possibility. After my nasty run in with the Colorado bear it definitely worried me.

Another time I was designing a non directional beacon, or NDB, for a village along the Yukon River. While looking over the site I had to walk down the Yukon River, and looking down I happened to find a real large tooth of a arctic elephant similar to the one my grand father had given me, from his days in Alaska. These artifacts are about the size of a gallon milk jug but with some strange markings.

Again, out in the Bush, on a remote and uninhabited island west of Sitka I was able to explore a World War II defense site. This place had been vacant for more than 60 years, and it was mostly underground. There was a living quarters area still full of bunk beds that looked like they were just waiting for the men to return at any moment. There were underground tunnels that ran to gun emplacements overlooking the open Pacific Ocean west of Sitka. Luckily I had a good flash light so I could walk through this spooky and dangerous place. There also was a separate building that was obviously a mess hall It appeared to almost be ready for a bunch of soldiers to come back from years ago and sit down and eat at any moment.

There was much more out in the Bush. On the mainland of Alaska I visited several sites for large "over the horizon" radio stations left over from the Cold War days. One I went through had a warehouse the size of a house elsewhere, and it was still full of Cold War electronic supplies of many types. Rack after rack of things like exotic radio tubes and similar components, actually thousands of items. There also was a very large parabolic reflector pointing east for contact with the military in the interior of Alaska and perhaps in the main part of the United States. Another spooky place, and there were lots more in Alaska.

Back home in Anchorage I bought a house that was a little different from anything I had ever see before. Two houses were built with a common wall between them but otherwise completely separate. The two were mirror images of each other having two bedrooms, a kitchen, living room and a bathroom. Mine also had a separate shed in the rear to store things, which was ideal for my electronic junk. Seeing the houses were built over a permanently frozen piece of glacial land each had a hollowed out space below as a form of insulation.

Shortly I became very friendly with a woman named Ann who had a teen aged son called Bill. Ann worked for a music store and Bill went to high school nearby. We got along quite well but Ann was not interested in marriage at all and Bill was the result of one of her earlier friendships. Anyway we were friends for quite a long time.

I got tired of living in a shared double house built on permafrost and found another more private house on a street closer to the edge of Anchorage and near a small lake. This house had just been put up for sale by a crippled veteran who had painted it a fluorescent blue color, and it was the talk of the neighborhood. At least it had three bedrooms, one for Bill, one for Ann and me, and one for my computer and ham radio equipment. But the first thing I did to this house was paint the exterior a good grayed color and got rid of the florescent paint. This was appreciated by the neighbors, I think.

Outside it was only a few hundred feet to a bluff which dropped off into the ocean. The little lake was a few hundred yards away in the other direction and Ann's Labrador dog loved to jump into the ice water and swim. In summer the lake beach would be full of children who would run out in the water for a quick swim also. In addition I put up a Yagi 20 meter radio ham radio antenna and was able to talk all over the world from here. I also became the president of the Anchorage ham radio club with perhaps five hundred members.

At this time one of the very active Anchorage ministers decided he was going to build a television station on the hillside near the city. It happened that a woman lived near his proposed TV station and she was extremely against this minister and his particular form of religion. She was strongly against his TV station and spent much time and effort promoting her ideas about getting rid of any antenna.

The woman convinced one of the City of Anchorage legal staff that there should be no antennas in Anchorage, because antennas meant the minister's TV station, and she was dead set against him. One of the cities lawyers was in total agreement too! They decided that they would pass a law that NO antennas of any kind would be allowed in Anchorage. I looked this over and found that there could be no ham radio antennas, no satellite telephone antennas to the lower United States, no police antennas, No fire department antennas. No ambulance antennas, none. They had no idea how this was going to put Anchorage back into the 1890 era and be very dangerous for all the people. I was able to spend a while discussing it on one of the local radio stations and explained what a disaster this special law was going to be for everyone, and it went away silently and completely.

Ann decided to buy a house for herself and Bill in a different part of Anchorage and get separated from me. Remarkable her new house was exactly the same dual format and floor plan as the one we all had been living in previously. And at the same time, 1997, I decided to sell my vacant house and retire from the FAA aviation organization.

I was not quite ready to leave Alaska rather I sold my house and took up residence in a motel in a town to the north of Anchorage about 40 miles. I searched for a cabin out in this area that would be suitable for a retired person living alone. I didn't find anything I felt was suitable.

One day I accidentally ran into an old friend in a parking lot and he said "we are going to sell our place at Big Lake, Alaska". His wife was crippled and it was about 80 steps down from his parking lot to the water front to get to his house on the lake. He already had another house on the lake, and best one without steps. Anyway I said "I know your place, and I'll buy it", we made a deal right there in the parking lot and I went off to see what I had made an offer for.

This was a partially completed two story house on the end of a peninsula in the very middle of Big Lake. The place also had a very good dock, a bath room, kitchen, large lower floor, and a huge upstairs bedroom. It also had an outbuilding my friend was trying to use, unsuccessfully, as a marine coffee stand. I made the deal, moved in and started completing his building. I put in a ceiling inside, then completed finishing the outside with insulation and lap sides of a neat style. Next I put in a very modern oil heater and a large oil tank up at the top of the hill above the house. This was a tremendous improvement over the wood stove he had been using to heat the house. I even installed a rug over the main part of the lower floor, and this covered the ax chop marks on the floor in front of the wood stove. It was now a modern home.

Outside I had room for my aluminum outboard motor boat in summer and for a couple of cars on the hill behind the house. In the winter, after the lake froze solid three feet deep, I could drive right up to the dock across the thick ice. I discovered there was a warm spring near the dock and the ice seldom got thick there but I avoided that area. I was going to heat the house with warm spring water, but the man who was to do the job got killed in a snow mobile accident and it never got completed, but at least I marked the warm spring.

Once during the cold midnight a truck was driving across the ice and discovered the warm spring. I looked out the window and could see just the front of the truck sticking up from the ice. Soon another truck with a friend came along and pulled the first truck out of the ice hole and the two men sat on the ice and drank the beer that had been in the sunken truck. In the morning the ice was covered with beer cans and the two trucks were gone. This was Alaska!

25

SMALL ISLAND IN THE ATLANTIC

Living at Big Lake, Alaska was fun but lonely. A big house echoed with my foot steps. I would go to the Methodist church on Sundays and often met women who were interested in me. One in particular who's husband had passed on built a good house out in the country invited me to visit. She was very much involved in local activities having lived in the area for many years. Somehow I did not quite fit into her plans and we did not get married.

Pretty soon I got on the Internet and found an organization that was promoting relations between lonely couples. This way I ran into Doreen MacCloud over in Calgary, Alberta, Canada. We conversed on the Internet and found we seemed to get along well and had common goals. I invited her to fly over to Anchorage and see what she thought of me. She said okay and she gave me the schedule of the flight. By some bad coincidence I happened to have that exact time taken by some very important meeting so I could not meet her plane. I asked one of my friends, a radio ham and a minister too, if he could pick Doreen up at the airport. I was remarkably lucky and he was able to get her at the airport and bring her out to Big Lake.

We almost immediately decided we were made for each other and would get married. Doreen had lived in the Canadian bush and had plenty of experience in remote places. She fit right in at Big Lake. Shortly we arranged to have a marriage in my friend's church in

Anchorage. Everything worked out very well and we lived together wonderfully until she died on April 19, 2016.

There were many other adventures after our marriage. To begin with Doreen wanted to go back to Nova Scotia where she had been born and where my great grandfather had lived. We arranged to put our Big Lake home up for sale with a Real Estate person and shortly it was sold. To move we had to get a ferry boat to take all our goods over to a dock where a truck could pick them up. This worked out alright and the goods were shipped over to a relative of Doreen's in Nova Scotia.

We went to Nova Scotia too by car and temporarily moved in to Doreen uncle's house trailer in a spare bed room. It was a vastly different situation than Alaska, much more civilized. For a couple of months we looked about for a living place. A real estate broker told us that he had a good place on Isle Madame, a small French speaking island off of the east side of very large Cape Breton Island. I really liked this offer as it connected nicely with my childhood French language experience. So we purchased a very good house at the town of D'Escouse on Isle Madame. We were lucky in that most of the people on our west side of the island also spoke English. Things went quite well for several years.

While living here on the island I was able to visit my great grand father's town of River John, Nova Scotia and see where he had owned a drug store. I also got to see his grave and the grave of a son killed in a boating accident. I also visited the Nova Scotia university my aunt Martha had attended. For me it was certainly a change from Alaska, but an exciting change, and one full of family history.

On Isle Madam, which might be translated from French as Queen Island, we ran into a bad neighbor. This man had sailed across the Pacific Ocean and around into the Atlantic Ocean and ended up buying the adjacent old house, actually several hundred feet away from us. He was what might be termed a "strange duck". Shortly after moving in he bought a tractor with a front blade for making roads. Soon he had built a road across our property to get to a piece of land he had also bought behind us.

I objected and took him to court where he said he was just protecting the history of Isle Madame, and his oh-so-noble run down house. Lie followed lie out of his mouth, but it was clear that he had used his tractor to build a road across our property, and remove the property markers, while doing it, but the judge only wanted me to have photographed him doing it. In the finish he did remove his illegal road, but nothing else.

All this bad neighborly activity burned Doreen up and she wanted to move back out west where she had several adult children living in British Columbia. So we sold our place at D'Escouse and moved west.

26

A CANADIAN RUSSIAN TOWN

MOST OF OUR household goods went by moving truck to a little town on the British Columbia border with eastern Washington state. This was a town settled partially by Russian Doukhobors. Here Doreen found a good two story house with about an acre or more land. It also had a barn where I could store the jet powered helicopter I had built in Nova Scotia.

In the town of Grand Forks we learned to like Russian food as the restaurants served excellent borscht and similar things from that country. We attended a Methodist church where the minister had a Russian name. From the back porch of our house we could even see into the United States and watch helicopters searching for dope smugglers. We never did see any caught. I will say the people here were remarkably friendly. Soon they even had me involved in the local "ham" radio club which did things like monitor bicycle races and such. Another thing they had me doing was teaching "ham" radio technology to a small but very active class of people interested in becoming "radio amateurs" and talking to the whole world.

Doreen however had itchy feet in this little town and wanted to move west even nearer to some of her daughter's, or to a son's vicinity, on Vancouver Island. For this reason we sold the house at Grand Forks, British Columbia and moved west to live temporarily with Doreen's son Steven at Campbell River, on very large Vancouver Island, on the Pacific Coast of British Columbia.

Steven's home here was in a house trailer on a private lot close to the Pacific Ocean between the Island and the main land of Canada. It was also close to two daughters, Nancy and Debby who were married to ministers in local churches on the island. Steven was in the automobile repair business on the island but was always looking for a way to improve his life style. Living with Steven was not exactly the life style I was looking forward to living, although he was entirely gracious in allowing us in his home.

My parents, Dr. Kurt Harden and Jennifer May Harden had quite recently moved to the small town of Sequim, Washington state, just south of where we were living on Vancouver Island by about 50 miles. They were in the process of purchasing a home there when my father became ill and died. At that point my mother moved back to Colorado and into a home for retired people run by a church organization called "The P.E.O" which mother had long been involved with in the Methodist Church.

She lived at the Church home in Colorado Springs for a period but shortly decided she did not like living in a compact apartment and she moved to a mid Florida town where two of her brother's and their wife's were living. Her stories to me about the good weather conditions on the Olympic Peninsula on the north west part of Washington state intrigued me as a place to live.

27

MOVING BACK TO USA

WE WENT SOUTH after a relatively short stay in Campbell River, BC, by way of the Motor Vessel Coho, a very large ocean going ferry boat. We sailed across the approximately 30 miles of the Juan de Fuca Straight, a salt water inlet between Canada and the United States and landed in Port Angeles, Washington just to the west of Seattle, Washington. From there we went to Sequim and started looking for a house in the country side which my mother had praised so highly.

I tried to find the house that interested my father and mother but was entirely unsuccessful. For about two weeks we were lead about the area of Sequim which the sales woman praised saying it was in the "rain shadow" of the mountains directly to the south. I could not find a place to compete with what we had in Canada. Plenty of good places, but not quite perfect. The homes were good but not exactly what I had hoped for. So we asked the sales woman to show us anything they had in the adjacent town of Port Angeles.

Going west ten miles or so was fascinating. We were now looking south of the only road and into a forest full of tremendously tall pine trees. We soon found a very good manufactured home, of about 2000 square feet, in the forest with a little over two acres of land and a small pond, plus a small herd of deer browsing on it's lawn. Out back the owner, who had recently died, had a large "bird house" of about 1000 square feet. She was raising large quantities of tropical birds for sale, and a few lived in the house too. Doreen figured we could get the bird poop removed with a pressure washer, and she was entirely right. We moved in and started cleaning. Doreen had plenty of experience in cleaning farm buildings, airports, ships, and such, and did it help. What a beautiful home it turned out to be.

Printed in the United States
By Bookmasters